GOSPEL SHAPED

OUTREACH

Handbook

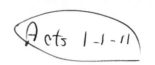
Acts 1-1-11

GOSPEL SHAPED

OUTREACH

Erik Raymond

thegoodbook
COMPANY

TGC THE GOSPEL
COALITION

Gospel Shaped Outreach Handbook
© The Gospel Coalition / The Good Book Company 2015. Reprinted 2015, 2017.

Published by:
The Good Book Company
Tel (US): 866 244 2165
Tel (UK): 0333 123 0880
Email (US): info@thegoodbook.com
Email (UK): info@thegoodbook.co.uk

Websites:
North America: www.thegoodbook.com
UK: www.thegoodbook.co.uk
Australia: www.thegoodbook.com.au
New Zealand: www.thegoodbook.co.nz

ISBN: 9781909919501 Printed in India

PRODUCTION TEAM:

AUTHOR:
Erik Raymond

**SERIES EDITOR FOR
THE GOSPEL COALITION:**
Collin Hansen

**SERIES EDITOR FOR
THE GOOD BOOK COMPANY:**
Tim Thornborough

**MAIN TEACHING SESSION
DISCUSSIONS:** Alison Mitchell

DAILY DEVOTIONALS:
Carl Laferton

BIBLE STUDIES:
Tim Thornborough

EDITORIAL ASSISTANTS:
Jeff Robinson (TGC), Rachel Jones (TGBC)

VIDEO EDITOR:
Phil Grout

PROJECT ADMINISTRATOR:
Jackie Moralee

EXECUTIVE PRODUCER:
Brad Byrd

DESIGN:
André Parker

CONTENTS

 **PREFACE**

GROWING A GOSPEL SHAPED CHURCH

The Gospel Coalition is a group of pastors and churches in the Reformed heritage who delight in the truth and power of the gospel, and who want the gospel of Christ crucified and resurrected to lie at the center of all we cherish, preach and teach.

We want churches called into existence by the gospel to be shaped by the gospel in their everyday life.

Through our fellowship, conferences, and online and printed media, we have sought to encourage pastors and church leaders to calibrate their lives around what is of first importance—the gospel of Christ. In these resources, we want to provide those same pastors with the tools to excite and equip church members with this mindset.

In our foundation documents, we identified five areas that should mark the lives of believers in a local fellowship:

1. Empowered corporate worship
2. Evangelistic effectiveness
3. Counter-cultural community
4. The integration of faith and work
5. The doing of justice and mercy

We believe that a church utterly committed to winsome and theologically substantial expository preaching, and that lives out the gospel in these areas, will display its commitment to dynamic evangelism, apologetics, and church planting. These gospel-shaped churches will emphasize repentance, personal renewal, holiness, and the wonderful life of the church as the body of Christ. At the same time, there will be engagement with the social structures of ordinary people, and cultural engagement with art, business, scholarship and government. The church will be characterized by firm devotion to the truth on the one hand, and by transparent compassion on the other.

The Gospel Coalition believes in the priority of the local church, and that the local church is the best place to discuss these five ministry drivers and decide how to integrate them into life and mission. So, while being clear on the biblical principles, these resources give space to consider what a genuine expression of a gospel-shaped church looks like for you in the place where God has put you, and with the people he has gathered into fellowship with you.

Through formal teaching sessions, daily Bible devotionals, group Bible studies and the regular preaching ministry, it is our hope and prayer that congregations will grow into maturity, and so honor and glorify our great God and Savior.

Don Carson
President

Tim Keller
Vice President

INTRODUCTION

Evangelicals, by definition, should believe in and practice evangelism. And yet many churches and Christians can lose sight of this primary goal for our life and work.

This is not an "evangelism course" like many others available. Often these courses will focus on the "how to" of evangelism, offering various techniques, programs and methods of outreach that individuals and churches can use. These can be incredibly helpful in giving us the confidence and skills to explain the good news to others.

But this course is different.

In the nine sessions in this curriculum, I have not sought to show you a particular way of explaining the gospel, but to lay strong biblical foundations for a broad and deep appreciation of the wonderful gospel of grace that we are called to understand, believe, rejoice in and proclaim to a waiting world.

As you work through the material, you will be able to share your own experiences, and benefit from the ideas and encouragement of your fellowship. You will also, no doubt, discover that you need more help and training in specific aspects of your witness for Christ in your community. This course will not be the last word on evangelism, for you or your church. But what I am aiming to do is to impress upon you, both as individuals and as a whole church, a deep conviction that God's mission of salvation in the world is also your mission; and that he is inviting you into the privilege of praying and working to advance his kingdom among your family, friends, neighbors, co-workers and community.

The Gospel Coalition identifies five hallmarks of a gospel-shaped church. One of those is evangelistic effectiveness, about which it says:

> *Because the gospel (unlike religious moralism) produces people who do not disdain those who disagree with them, a truly gospel–centered church should be filled with members who winsomely address people's hopes and aspirations with Christ and his saving work. We have a vision for a*

church that sees conversions of rich and poor, highly educated and less educated, men and women, old and young, married and single, and all races. We hope to draw highly secular and postmodern people, as well as reaching religious and traditional people. Because of the attractiveness of its community and the humility of its people, a gospel–centered church should find people in its midst who are exploring and trying to understand Christianity. It must welcome them in hundreds of ways. It will do little to make them "comfortable" but will do much to make its message understandable. In addition to all this, gospel–centered churches will have a bias toward church planting as one of the most effective means of evangelism there is.

It is my prayer that as you work through this curriculum, you and your church will become more and more the community and people that you are called to be: a fellowship that is effective at, and excited about, bringing the gospel to those around you.

Erik Raymond

HOW TO USE GOSPEL SHAPED OUTREACH

MAIN TEACHING SESSION This session combines watching short talks on a DVD or listening to "live" talks with times for discussion. These prompt you to think about what you have heard and how it might apply to your church and cultural context. Bear in mind that there is not necessarily a "right answer" to every question!

DEVOTIONALS Each session comes with six daily personal devotionals. These look at passages that are linked to the theme of the Main Teaching Session, and are for you to read and meditate on at home through the week after the session. You may like to do them in addition to or instead of your usual daily devotionals, or use them to begin such a practice.

JOURNAL As you reflect on what you have learned as a group and in your personal devotionals, use this page to record the main truths that have struck you, things you need to pray about, and issues you'd like to discuss further or questions you'd like to ask.

BIBLE STUDY As part of this curriculum, your church may be running weekly Bible Studies as well as the Main Teaching Sessions. These look more closely at a passage and help you focus on an aspect of the Main Teaching Session. If your church is not using this part of the curriculum, you could work through it on your own or with another church member.

SERMON NOTES Your church's preaching program may be following this curriculum; space has been provided for you to make notes on these sermons in your Handbook.

SESSION 1:

HOW ARE WE DOING?

WHAT IS GOSPEL-SHAPED EVANGELISM, AND HOW SHOULD THAT MOLD OUR CHURCH? THESE ARE THE QUESTIONS WE WILL BE CONSIDERING IN THESE SESSIONS. FIRST, WE NEED TO SEE WHAT EVANGELISM ACTUALLY IS; THEN UNDERSTAND WHAT AN EVANGELISTIC CHURCH CULTURE WOULD LOOK LIKE; AND FINALLY REFLECT UPON WHERE WE ARE AT IN OUR OWN CHURCH AND LIVES.

HOW ARE WE DOING?

Discuss

What comes into your mind when you hear the word "evangelism"?

_____

_____

_____

_____

▶ **WATCH DVD 1.1 OR LISTEN TO TALK 1.1**

_____

_____

_____

_____

_____

_____

_____

Discuss

"Over time, evangelism becomes less of a reflex and more of a challenge."
Do you agree? Have you experienced a gradual decline in your own personal
evangelism? What factors do you think might have contributed to this?

_____

_____

_____

👉 ROMANS 10:13-15

13 For "everyone who calls on the name of the Lord will be saved."
14 How then will they call on him in whom they have not believed? And how are they to believe in him of whom they have never heard? And how are they to hear without someone preaching? 15 And how are they to preach unless they are sent? As it is written, "How beautiful are the feet of those who preach the good news!"

What needs to happen before someone becomes a Christian ("calls on the name of the Lord")? List the steps from the passage.

_____

_____

_____

_____

_____

In verse 15, Paul describes evangelism as "beautiful." Why do we often forget that evangelism is like this?

_____

_____

_____

_____

▶ WATCH DVD 1.2 OR LISTEN TO TALK 1.2

_____

_____

_____

_____

_____

_____

_____

_____

Discuss

☞ EPHESIANS 6:18-20

18 To that end keep alert with all perseverance, making supplication for all the saints, 19 and also for me, that words may be given to me in opening my mouth boldly to proclaim the mystery of the gospel, 20 for which I am an ambassador in chains, that I may declare it boldly, as I ought to speak.

1. PRAY

Why do you think Paul asks them to pray for words and for boldness?

_____

_____

_____

When was the last time you asked someone to pray for your faithfulness in evangelism?

_____

_____

_____

Think of someone you can ask to pray for you and your faithfulness to "declare it boldly."

_____

_____

2. TAKE

When Paul and Silas were in prison, the earthquake gave them the opportunity to escape—but they didn't. Instead, they took the opportunity to tell their jailer the gospel (Acts 16:23-34).

Honestly, what do you think your response would have been if you had been Paul or Silas? Would you have taken the opportunity to escape?

Can you recall an example when God gave you an evangelistic opportunity in a surprising way? Did you take it? If not, what stopped you?

3. MAKE

"The only qualification for evangelism is to be a Christian."
Does this surprise you? How is it an exciting challenge?

What did you hear on the DVD / in the talk that particularly motivated you to tell people the gospel message?

Think of two people you would like to share the gospel with in the next month. Discuss how you could make opportunities to do this. Commit to praying regularly for one another, and to asking each other how this is going.

_____

_____

_____

_____

Pray

Pray for your church as it works through this curriculum. Pray that you will grow in your excitement about the gospel, that you will encourage one another, and that you will learn together what it means to be a church that has a culture of evangelism.

Pray for each other individually that you will make opportunities to share the gospel with the two people you listed above, and that you will have the words to say and the boldness to say them.

Pray that you will share the Lord's compassion for those who are hopeless and helpless without Jesus; and that you will be jealous for God's glory.

DAILY BIBLE DEVOTIONALS

This week our daily readings are focused on Acts 17, and the apostle Paul's evangelism in the ancient Greek city of Athens.

Day 1

ACTS 17:16-17

Paul is alone in Athens, the intellectual and philosophical center of the Roman world, having been chased out of Philippi, Thessalonica and Berea by opponents of the gospel.

Q: *How does Paul feel, and why (v 16)?*

Q: *How does this cause him to act (v 17)?*

If we are driven by a longing for Christ's glory, we will see, feel and do as Paul did. We will not notice the buildings or politics of our cities so much as the idolatry. We will not feel complacent or comfortable; rather, we will be distressed that Jesus is ignored. And our passion for Christ in a place of idols will cause us to speak out.

Q: *Do you see as Paul did? Do you feel as he did?*

Q: *What will change today if you do?*

PRAY: *Lord, make me jealous for your glory. Give me eyes to see as Paul did, a heart to feel what he did, and a mouth to speak as he did.*

Day 2

ACTS 17:17-18

Q: *What groups does Paul speak to?*

Q: *What are the equivalents of those groups in your culture today?*

Religious God-fearing people need to hear about "Jesus and the resurrection" (v 18), for our religious duties cannot save us. Ordinary, busy people need to hear about the Lord Jesus as they go about their lives, for all lives will end. And academic people need to hear about him too, because human wisdom cannot fathom, far less achieve, immortality.

Wherever you go today, and whoever you meet today, the resurrection will be gloriously good news, and urgently needed news.

Q: *Think about the non-believers you will likely meet today. How can you make and take an opportunity to tell them about the risen Jesus?*

PRAY: *Lord, thank you that the gospel is good news for everyone. Please enable me to share Jesus with someone, or several people, today.*

Day 3

ACTS 17:19-23

Paul is speaking to the ruling council of Athens: one of the most learned, and intimidating, gatherings in the world.

Q: *What does Paul "perceive" about the Athenians (v 22)?*

Q: *What are these well-educated men totally ignorant of?*

Q: *What does Paul promise (v 23)?*

If we wish to share the gospel with people, we must connect the gospel to people. Paul meets these men where they are at: worshiping "the unknown god." He connects to their belief systems, and then offers the gospel as the answer to their ignorance—the God they admit they do not know has made himself knowable.

To witness well, we must "see": we must listen to people, understand them and know their hopes and fears. And we must "proclaim": invite them to discover the One who makes sense of life.

Q: *Think about one non-Christian you know well. How does the good news connect to their hopes or fears? How is it good news for them specifically?*

PRAY: *Lord, let me see how the gospel connects to the beliefs, dreams and fears of those around me.*

Day 4

ACTS 17:24-28

Paul begins his gospel address by proclaiming who God is, and who we are.

Q: *Who is God? What has he done?*

Q: *Why did God put people in the places and times in which they live (v 27)?*

We often think God needs us: he requires our service for his work to be done. Verse 25 reminds us that this is far from true! In fact, we need God, and he graciously allows us to be part of his world, and part of his purposes. And in his sovereignty, he has placed everyone just where he wants them. You will not meet anyone by accident. No interaction will be chance.

Why has God placed people where he has? Because he is at work to reach out to people so that they may reach out to him (v 27). The reason your neighbor lives where they do is so they might be reached for the gospel; the reason you live where you do is so that you might be the way God reaches out to them. This transforms your view of your day! It makes your everyday interactions far more exciting!

Q: *Is this how you view each day? What will change if you do?*

PRAY: *Father, your sovereign goodness and purposes are amazing! Please use me as part of them today.*

Day 5

ACTS 17:29-31

Athens is full of idol-statues (v 16). How ridiculous, Paul says, to worship something you can make! It is like thinking you can create your own parent (v 29)!

Q: *What does Paul declare will happen in the future (v 31)?*

God has written a day on his calendar: *judgment*. It is a day all people everywhere need to be prepared for. The event is certain, proved by the resurrection. The name of the Judge is definite, identified by that resurrection.

Q: *What action does the resurrection in the past, and Judgment Day in the future, call for (v 30)?*

Repentance means turning from self-rule to Christ's rule, and from self-reliance to Christ-reliance. It is humbling, but also liberating; and it turns Judgment Day from a dead end into a doorway. So calling someone to repent is both a direct challenge to them, and a wonderful invitation for them.

Q: *Is there someone you need to call to repent, gently but firmly?*

PRAY: *Lord, thank you that you are my Judge and my Savior. Give me grace to repent where and when I need to. And give me courage to invite others to repent where and when I can.*

Day 6

It is easy to have a rose-tinted view of the apostle Paul's evangelism—that he preached in the morning, hundreds repented by noon, a church was founded in the afternoon, and Paul then wrote a book of Scripture in the evening. In reality, Paul's experience of evangelism was much more like ours…

ACTS 17:32-34

Q: *What two responses are there to the idea of a resurrection (v 32)?*

Q: *What happens to a few of the second group (v 34)?*

Q: *What can we learn about evangelism here?*

The pessimistic view is that after all that time and effort, the results were sparse amid the sneering. But look again with a gospel focus; what a glorious result! Several miracles occurred! Several eternal destinations were utterly changed! We must not be surprised when our witness is met with sneering; we should be expecting that sometimes it will provoke interest; and we will be thrilled if and when we see the miracle of belief in Jesus, and know we had the privilege of being used by God. Paul was a man like us—and so we can witness like him.

PRAY: *Father, help me to witness faithfully and fully, leaving the results to you.*

 **JOURNAL**

What I've learned or been particularly struck by this week…

Acts 1:.. what we need in order to spread the gospel.
1. instruction from Jesus (V. 1)
2. evidence (V.3)
3. Power (V.5)
4. The Command (v.8)

What I want to change in my perspectives or actions as a result of this week…

Things I would like to think about more or discuss with others at my church…

Discuss

Many businesses list their main aims as a "mission statement" to help them keep focused when making decisions, and to order their priorities.

Talk about some of these that you know—perhaps a company that you have worked for. What happens when an organization does not have specific aims or priorities?

☛ READ ACTS 1:1-11

¹ In the first book, O Theophilus, I have dealt with all that Jesus began to do and teach...

1. What is exciting about the word "began" in Acts 1:1?

_____

_____

2. What does Jesus want the disciples to do, and why (v 4-8)? Why might they have felt terrified by this command?

_____

_____

_____

_____

3. What are the suggestions in the passage that Jesus' plans for his people are different from what the disciples expected (v 6-8)?

_____

_____

_____

4. Jesus speaks of witnesses going "to the end of the earth" (v 8). How does this show that he had in mind not only those he was speaking to, but all his followers, throughout the ages?

5. What did the first disciples need in order to be able to spread the gospel (v 2, 3, 5, 8)? What would go wrong if one of these was missing?

Do we need anything different?

6. So how does Jesus work in the world today to spread the gospel?

7. What is the implication of what the angels say in verse 11?
   What were the apostles still hanging onto, and what should they have been doing? How can we be similarly confused?

Apply

FOR YOURSELF: Where would you list "telling the good news about Jesus to others" on the list of your personal priorities? What do you struggle with most—the desire to witness, the words to say, or the boldness to say them?

_____

_____

_____

_____

FOR YOUR CHURCH: Look over your church calendar of events. What do you conclude about how important outreach is to you as a church family at the moment? How are you praying for, taking and making opportunities to share the gospel as a church together?

_____

_____

_____

_____

Pray

FOR THE GROUP: Ask God to give you opportunities, the words and boldness to speak about the gospel of Christ.

FOR YOUR WHOLE CHURCH: Pray that working through this curriculum would be a constructive exercise for your church. Pray for unity and for your leaders. And pray that the end result will be that your church is more committed to gospel-shaped outreach.

SERMON NOTES

Bible passage: Date: *These are all Selfish.*

Obstacles to Outreach —

1. What does God want for me in my life?
2. do I have the personality gifts or talents?
         Peter, Timothy, Mary, so not necessary
3. I feel awkward — will I mess up
4. I am scared — will I be made fun of
5. I do not have time ... to save people!?
6. Don't just convert people but make disciples!

SESSION 2:
WHO IS JESUS?

WE'VE SEEN THAT EVANGELISM IS THE ACTION OF
TELLING PEOPLE THE GOSPEL; AND THAT AS A CHURCH
WE NEED TO BE COMMITTED TO PRAYING FOR, MAKING,
AND TAKING OPPORTUNITIES TO TALK ABOUT THE
GOSPEL MESSAGE. THAT MESSAGE CENTERS ON JESUS.
BUT... JUST WHO *IS* JESUS?
IN THIS SESSION, WE'LL CONSIDER WHAT ASPECTS
OF HIS IDENTITY WE NEED TO UNDERSTAND AND BE
EXCITED BY, SO THAT WE'LL BE ABLE AND WILLING TO
TELL OTHERS WHAT THEY NEED TO HEAR.

WHO IS JESUS?

Discuss

If you asked a random set of people at your local shopping mall who they thought Jesus was or is, what different answers would you get?

_____

_____

_____

_____

Which of these views do you think is growing in popularity?

_____

_____

_____

_____

_____

▶ **WATCH DVD 2.1 OR LISTEN TO TALK 2.1**

_____

_____

_____

_____

_____

_____

_____

Discuss

The Bible reveals to us that God is a Trinity—a Tri (three) Unity—Father, Son and Holy Spirit.

Is the Trinity a subject you would bring up in an evangelistic conversation? Why or why not?

_____

_____

_____

_____

"Jesus is fully God—100%—and wholly man—100%."
Which of these do you find hardest to grasp? Why is it vital for the gospel message that both of these things are true?

_____

_____

_____

_____

▶ **WATCH DVD 2.2 OR LISTEN TO TALK 2.2**

_____

_____

_____

_____

_____

_____

_____

_____

Discuss

1. Jesus is God in the flesh.
2. Jesus is the resurrected King.
3. Jesus is the truth-telling Lord.
4. Jesus is the sin-bearing Savior.
5. Jesus is the only way.

What is the good news for us in each of these statements?

Which of these came across to you most powerfully when you first heard the gospel?

Are there any you only heard/appreciated later on? What impact did that have on you?

"The gospel message, at its most simple, is this—Jesus is Lord."

From what you have heard in this session, how might you unpack the phrase "Jesus is Lord" to explain what it means?

_____

_____

_____

_____

_____

_____

_____

_____

_____

_____

You could use the verses below to help you.

ROMANS 10:9

If you confess with your mouth that Jesus is Lord and believe in your heart that God raised him from the dead, you will be saved.

COLOSSIANS 1:19

For in him all the fullness of God was pleased to dwell.

JOHN 1:3

All things were made through him, and without him was not any thing made that was made.

MATTHEW 1:21

You shall call his name Jesus, for he will save his people from their sins.

"If we don't talk about Jesus, we are adding noise to a confused conversation." Look at the following statements. How could you turn these into conversations about Jesus?

"All religions are the same, so it doesn't matter which you believe."

_____

_____

_____

"I try to treat people the way I'd want to be treated. I figure I've lived an OK life."

_____

_____

_____

"My friend says that when we die, we come back as someone else. I hope I'll be rich next time."

_____

_____

_____

Pray

Look again at the list on page 33. Thank Jesus for being each one of these things.

Think of the person who first told you the gospel message or helped you understand it more fully. Thank God for bringing that person into your life so that you could know the truth about the Lord Jesus.

Pray that you will grow in your knowledge and love of Jesus, and that you will want to share that joy with other people.

DAILY BIBLE DEVOTIONALS

We won't be excited about speaking of Jesus till we have marveled at Jesus. This week, we will wonder at the aspects of Jesus' identity shared in the main session.

Day 1

Everyone accepts someone's advice as their foundation. We all build our lives on someone's words. The question is: *Whose?*

MATTHEW 7:24-28

Q: *How can we build our lives on a solid rock that cannot be shaken (v 24-25)?*

Q: *What is the other option (v 26-27)?*

Advice is offered everywhere, but truth is in very short supply. It is so easy to build an impressive-looking life that is washed away by the storms of recession, heartbreak or illness. And every life will be washed away by the flood of final judgment… unless it is built on the rock of Jesus' word. It is hard to build on Christ's words—they undermine the world's assumptions (read 5:38-48; 6:1-4, 19-34). But it is such a relief to know we are building on material that will support us. Jesus is the **truth-telling Lord**: his words will never fail us.

Q: *Do you see Jesus' commands as a relief and joy to follow? Why/why not?*

PRAY: *Lord, thank you that your words are true. Thank you that I can know the joy of building on solid rock.*

Day 2

MATTHEW 8:23-27

Q: *What do the disciples face, and what do they fear (v 24-25)?*

Q: *What is Jesus doing in the boat (v 24)? What does he do to the storm (v 26)?*

Q: *How do the disciples respond (v 27)? What is the answer to their question?*

Here is **God in the flesh**. Few things remind us of our vulnerable humanity more than our need for sleep—and Jesus slept (v 24). But nothing points to unfathomable power more than Jesus' command of the winds and sea— the "great calm" (v 26) shouts of divinity. The disciples got into that boat with a man; they left it suspecting they were in the presence of God. And wonderfully, this God-man is willing to use his power to calm our fears and to save us from perishing. He chooses to use his divine power to serve his people. Our response must surely be to "marvel" (v 27).

PRAY: *Echo the words of this hymn:*
"I stand amazed in the presence / Of Jesus the Nazarene / And wonder how he could love me / A sinner, condemned, unclean."
Thank you Jesus, my God.

Day 3

Q: *Imagine someone said to you: "Why is Jesus unique?" What would you say?*

MATTHEW 9:14-17

Q: *How does Jesus answer the question about fasting (v 15)?*

God describes himself in the Old Testament as his people's Bridegroom (eg: Isaiah 62:5; Hosea 2:14-20). And of course, there can only be one Bridegroom. So Jesus is making a staggering claim to an **exclusive position**: that he is God.

Jesus came into the world to be the fulfillment of true Old Testament religion and the subversion of all man-made religion. He is not looking for subjects focused on dutiful performance; he wants followers who enjoy his friendship. So Jesus will never be satisfied with being used to patch up our old lives; nor can he be contained by our old lives. No—he came to bring a whole new life! He will be our everything—or he will be nothing to us, and do nothing for us. Following Jesus will not bring us comfort in this life; but it will bring us joy. There is only one Bridegroom; and his name is Jesus.

Q: *Are there ways that you're trying to hang on to your old life, rather than enjoying newness of life with Jesus?*

PRAY: *Lord, thank you for making me part of your Bride, your church. Help me never to treat you as a patch on my old life, but as the everything of my new life.*

Day 4

Here is one of the most moving parts of Scripture. It must cause us to adore the man praying in a garden hours before his death.

MATTHEW 26:36-46

Q: *Read Isaiah 51:17 and Jeremiah 25:15-16. What is "this cup" (Matthew 26:39)? How does Jesus feel about drinking it (v 38-39)?*

Q: *What are Jesus' friends doing while he is in such distress (v 40, 43)? How do you react to their conduct?*

It's impossible to overstate the magnitude of this. The perfect, sinless, holy Son of God begins to taste what it will be for him to face wrath like a sinner. He takes a sip from the cup of God's righteous anger, and he recoils from it: "Let this cup pass from me." And yet he resolves to drink it to its dregs: "Not as I will, but as you will." Why? So that you and I wouldn't have to drink any of it, ever. We who have said to God: "Not as you will, but as I will"—we who have failed Jesus, just as his disciples did—we deserve the cup. And Jesus drank it for *us*. He is our **sin-bearing Savior**. We cannot hope to fully understand these events. We can only describe them, believe them, and be led to worship by them.

PRAY: *"For me it was in the garden / He prayed: 'Not my will, but thine.' / He had not tears for his own griefs / But sweat drops of blood for mine."* Thank you, Lord, so, so much. I love you.

Day 5

The Truth-teller has been brought down by lies. The Storm-commander has succumbed to death's claims. The One who claimed to be the unique God has died as just another common criminal. The story is over…

MATTHEW 28:1-10

We do not merely love a crucified man (v 5). We worship a **risen King**, who always keeps his promises (v 6).

Q: *How do the first witnesses of the resurrection feel (v 8)?*

Q: *When they meet Jesus, how does Jesus tell them not to feel (v 10)?*

Because Jesus is the resurrected King, the story continues beyond his grave. But what is our part in it? If Jesus had not first been crucified for us, the resurrection must make us tremble (v 4). We need to hear Jesus say to *us*: "Do not be afraid" (v 10). Together, the wooden cross and empty tomb remove all reason to fear, and give us great joy. Whatever happens today, a day will come when we "will see him" (v 7)—not in Galilee in AD33, but in heaven for eternity.

Q: *What fear will you ask the risen Jesus to replace with joy right now?*

PRAY: *King Jesus, thank you that you are alive. Give me the joy of knowing this in my heart as well as my head. Show me how to worship at your feet, wherever my feet may take me today.*

Day 6

The Christian life does not consist of knowing *about* Jesus, but of knowing *him*. Our devotional lives must never become an intellectual pursuit; rather, they are to be an act of adoration, a pursuit of our Bridegroom—our great resurrected King, truth-telling Lord, sin-bearing Savior and humble, human-clothed God. It is *this* Jesus who commands us at the end of the Gospel of Matthew: "Make disciples of all nations" (28:18). And because it is *this* Jesus who calls us to spend our lives making worshipers of him, evangelism becomes not a burden or a duty, but a joy and a privilege.

If you wish your lips to speak about Christ to others, then teach them to sing about Christ to yourself:

"How marvelous! How wonderful!
And my song shall ever be:
How marvelous! How wonderful!
Is my Savior's love for me!"
(Charles H. Gabriel)

Q: *Which of this week's devotional passages most moved you to worship Jesus? Re-read it, and adore him all over again.*

Q: *Which passage are you struggling to remember as you look back over the week? Re-read it now, and pray that God's Spirit would write its truths on your heart.*

PRAY: *Lord Jesus, help me to marvel at you more today than I did yesterday, and less than I will tomorrow.*

 JOURNAL

What I've learned or been particularly struck by this week…

_____

_____

_____

_____

_____

_____

What I want to change in my perspectives or actions as a result of this week…

_____

_____

_____

_____

_____

_____

Things I would like to think about more or discuss with others at my church…

_____

_____

_____

_____

_____

_____

BIBLE STUDY

Discuss

What popular films or TV portrayals of Jesus have you seen recently? How do you think these have helped or hindered our understanding of Jesus' true identity and mission?

What value (if any) do you think there is in such attempts to portray Christ?

☛ READ COLOSSIANS 1:15-23

15 He is the image of the invisible God, the firstborn of all creation...

1. Notice the number of times that Paul uses the words "all," "everything" and "fullness." What big point is he making in this passage?

_____

_____

_____

2. Which verses show that Jesus is fully God, and which show that he is also fully man? How would you explain to someone who isn't a Christian that Jesus is the "image" of God?

_____

_____

_____

3. Most people in the west think the universe came about by chance, and is sustained by the laws of physics. What would Paul say about that (see v 15-17)?

_____

_____

4. What is the natural state of human beings (v 21, see also v 13)? How have you seen this in your own life, and in the lives of people you know?

_____

_____

_____

5. How does Jesus' death on the cross deal with this (v 20, 22)?

_____

_____

How would you explain to someone what it means that the cross brings peace?

_____

_____

_____

6. What happens when someone responds to the message about Jesus (v 20-23, see also v 13)?

_____

_____

So why is it such a privilege to be a "minister" or servant of the gospel (v 23)?

_____

_____

_____

7. How should people respond to Christ (v 23)? Who is the "you" Paul is addressing in this verse?

_____

_____

Apply

FOR YOURSELF: The gospel message is all about Jesus—who he is and what he has done. What are some of the less offensive aspects of the Christian life that we are tempted to talk about instead of Jesus? How can we help ourselves and each other to talk more about Jesus?

FOR YOUR CHURCH: Look back over the five aspects of who Jesus is and what he has done on page 33. Do you think your church emphasizes one of the aspects over the others? Are there any aspects of him that you might be in danger of neglecting? Why is that—and what is the remedy?

Pray

Spend some time worshiping the Lord together in words—using the passage as a basis for your thanks and praise.

FOR THE GROUP: Ask God to give you each a bigger vision for who Jesus is and what he has done for you.

FOR YOUR WHOLE CHURCH: Pray that working through this curriculum would be a constructive exercise for your church. Pray for unity and for your leaders. And pray that the end result will be that your church is more committed to gospel-shaped outreach.

SERMON NOTES

Bible passage: Date:

SESSION 3:

WHO ARE WE?

WE'VE CONSIDERED WHO JESUS IS – GOD IN THE FLESH,
THE RESURRECTED KING, THE TRUTH-TELLING LORD,
THE SIN-BEARING SAVIOR AND THE ONLY WAY TO BE
RIGHT WITH GOD. THE HEART OF THE GOSPEL MESSAGE
IS JESUS. NOW WE MOVE ON TO LOOK AT THE HEARTS
OF THE MESSENGERS – US, AND OUR CHURCH. IT IS NOT
ONLY JESUS' IDENTITY THAT WE NEED TO APPRECIATE –
IT IS OURS, TOO.

As Jesus was sent by God, we need to also stay on mission to transform people.

WHO ARE WE?

Discuss

Talk about any missionaries you know. What do you imagine their lives are like from day to day?

We are all missionaries — to teach about Jesus

Can you come up with a simple definition of what a missionary is?

▶ **WATCH DVD 3.1 OR LISTEN TO TALK 3.1**

Discuss

What did Roger say was the most discouraging thing on the mission field?
If you were supporting a missionary who was like this, what would you say to
them?

_____

_____

_____

_____

_____

_____

*"Believers in the church should see themselves as a missionary family—and the
family business is making and training disciples."*
How did you react to this statement?

_____

_____

_____

_____

_____

What are some of the reasons why individual believers and whole churches can lose
their focus on reaching out to others?

_____

_____

_____

_____

_____

▶ WATCH DVD 3.2 OR LISTEN TO TALK 3.2

_____
_____
_____
_____
_____
_____
_____
_____
_____
_____
_____

Discuss

"The enemy of evangelism is selfishness."
In what ways have you seen this to be true in your own life?

_____
_____
_____
_____

"Loving service is the heart of evangelism."
How would things look different in our own lives and in our church if we were
motivated by loving service, rather than selfishness?

_____
_____
_____
_____

MATTHEW 28:19

"Go therefore and make disciples of all nations."

"All nations" includes **your** nation, so discuss the same questions that Erik asked his friend: *"What would change about your life if you did your current job as a missionary in another country? What changes would you make if you had been sent to a foreign country, and given a job, a house and the mandate to be a missionary and reach those people?"*

- How would you spend your time?

_____

_____

_____

- How would you pray?

_____

_____

_____

- What types of relationships would you pursue?

_____

_____

_____

- How would you read the news?

_____

_____

_____

● What would you think of your neighbors?

_____

_____

_____

● How would you talk to the cashiers at the local supermarket?

_____

_____

_____

● What would you be listening for in your community?

_____

_____

_____

What practical things can we do to keep showing each other and encouraging each other that we are part of a missionary family?

_____

_____

_____

_____

Pray

Pray for the missionaries you thought about at the beginning of this session. Now pray for yourselves as missionaries, and your church as a missionary family. Look again at the answers you gave to the final question above. Ask God to help you put these things into action.

DAILY BIBLE DEVOTIONALS

What part does church play in evangelism? What does it mean for believers to live together as a missionary family? 1 Peter sheds light on these questions…

Day 1

1 PETER 1:22 – 2:3

Q: *How are Christians to treat each other, and not treat each other (1:22; 2:1)?*

Q: *How are people born into this family of believers (1:23)?*

The Greek word translated "sincere" (v 22) means abundantly, gushingly. This kind of love makes us vulnerable, and requires sacrifice. It is the kind of love God pours out on us! And we are to love each other with this kind of love. To do this, we need to keep tasting the Lord through his eternal word (2:3), rather than gorging ourselves on the sinful spiritual junk food of 2:1. This kind of love blesses believers and attracts outsiders. **Read John 13:34-35.**

Q: *Have you realized that a missional church must be a sincerely loving family? What will this look like for you today and this week?*

Q: *How does 2:1 challenge you?*

PRAY: *Lord, thank you that I have been born again, into your eternal family. Help me to love my brothers and sisters with the kind of love you show me.*

Day 2

Q: *What is the most impressive building you have ever seen?*

1 PETER 2:4-5

Q: *Verse 4 describes Jesus as a building block. How does God view him?*

Q: *What happens to people as they put their faith in Jesus (v 5)?*

Peter wants to hold up a biblical lens for you to view your church through. As we look with a biblical focus, we see that God has embarked on a worldwide, eternal building project—and the stones he's using are people: me and you. God takes us, whoever and whatever we are, and builds us into something magnificent—a building where he puts his presence, and is delighted to receive worship. What is the most impressive building you have ever seen? We are.

Q: *How does this excite you about being a member of your church?*

PRAY: *Thank God for your local church and the living stones he has built into it. Pray for a renewed excitement about, and commitment to, your church.*

Day 3

1 PETER 2:6-8

Q: *What has God done, and what does he promise (v 6)?*

Q: *What problem do those who choose to build their lives without Jesus have (v 7)?*

Q: *How has chapter 2 up to this point shown us that it is an "honor" to believe in and build on Christ?*

We stumble over Christ because we want to be our own cornerstone. We want to build our own empire, centered around us. But if we are not built into God's church— accepting the privilege of being a stone connected to *the* chosen stone—all we manage to build for ourselves will one day be reduced to rubble. There is only one structure in this world that will still stand in 10,000,000 years. It is the church. You never, ever need to regret or be ashamed of being part of what God is constructing. You will eternally love being a tiny part of his cosmic building, rather than eternally regret being at the center of your own tiny empire of rubble.

Q: *To what extent does your attitude to church make plain to those around you that the church is God's eternal building project?*

PRAY: *Father, thank you that you have declared that Christ is the cornerstone. Thank you for building me onto him.*

Day 4

We have seen what church *is*. But what does church *do*?

1 PETER 2:9-10

These verses are saturated with Old Testament descriptions of Israel, God's ancient people. **Read Exodus 19:5-6; Isaiah 43:20-21; Hosea 1:8-10.** Peter says: *Church, this is now who you are, and what you do.*

The role of a priest was to speak to God about people, and to speak to people about God. In one sense, Christ is the only priest now. But in another, all Christians are priests. The church is a royal priesthood, with the job of praying to God for people's salvation, and speaking to people about God's salvation.

Q: *What does the people of God today— the church—exist to proclaim (v 9)?*

We do not only do this as individuals, but as family. We are a missionary family together, not just a family of individual missionaries. If we are serious about evangelism, we'll be serious about church, and about ensuring that every aspect of church life declares God's excellencies to those who don't know him.

Q: *How is your church doing this? Are there areas that need thinking about?*

PRAY: *Lord God, help us to declare your excellencies to our community as we celebrate them with each other.*

Day 5

Our lives, as well as our lips, need to proclaim the excellencies of our great God.

1 PETER 2:11

Q: *How does Peter tell us to see ourselves?*

We are on a short-term missions trip. Heaven is our home, and we are on our way there. We're passing through, and so we love our future more than our present.

Q: *What must we do until we get home, does Peter say?*

Our desires are natural; but this does not mean that they are noble, nor that we should listen to and obey them. Our grudges war against our compassion. Our ambitions undermine our contentment. Our lusts strike at our purity. There is a battle going on, and the battlefield is us. And we win the battle as we say "no" to the desires which we know are very natural, and not at all noble.

Q: *Are there times when a failure to war against your desires undermines your ability to declare God's excellencies to those around you?*

Q: *How does this motivate you to keep battling those desires? What will you seek to think about in their place?*

PRAY: *Father, I'm on my way home. Help me to fight my battle today.*

Day 6

Q: *What reputation does your church have? What are you known for?*

1 PETER 2:12

Q: *What should characterize our lives?*

"Honorable" means honorable to God, first and foremost. God, not those around us, decides what "good deeds" are. We are to seek to please our Father before we seek to impress our neighbors.

Q: *But what effect will living his way have on those who live around us?*

The media increasingly equate Christian beliefs with evil. The conduct of the local church is the way that such claims will be undermined, and such views reversed. The end of verse 12 likely refers to people realizing their stereotypes of Christianity are wrong, as they see the glory of God in the beauty of real Christian lives. As the local church reflects God's glory, they begin to want to enjoy and praise God themselves. It is the witness of a godly life that will change voices that criticize Christians into ones that give glory to God.

Q: *How can your church be increasingly known for its good, godly deeds? What part could you play in this?*

PRAY: *Lord, we long for you to be glorified. Show us how to live in a way that glorifies you, and that brings others to glorify you, too.*

JOURNAL

What I've learned or been particularly struck by this week…

_____
_____
_____
_____
_____
_____

What I want to change in my perspectives or actions as a result of this week…

_____
_____
_____
_____
_____
_____

Things I would like to think about more or discuss with others at my church…

_____
_____
_____
_____
_____
_____

BIBLE STUDY

Discuss

"The church is…" How might people finish that sentence if you asked a random selection of strangers in the street? How would *you* finish that sentence?

READ ACTS 2:42-47

> 42 *And they devoted themselves to the apostles' teaching and the fellowship, to the breaking of bread and the prayers…"*

1. Pick out some key characteristics of the church that Jesus formed by his Holy Spirit in the first few months after Pentecost.

2. What would it have been like to be part of that first church? What would particularly attract you to join it?

   Do you feel the same way about your own church? Why or why not?

3. What was the cause of the spectacular growth of this church family?

4. How did their life together support and complement the preaching of the good news about Jesus?

_____

_____

But the admiration of the church didn't last for long. Acts 3 – 4 recounts how, after Peter and John had spectacularly healed a disabled man in the name of Jesus, they were arrested, flogged, and warned not to speak about Christ any more. This was their response…

READ ACTS 4:18-31

5. When they are threatened, what do they do in response? Do you think this was easy for them?

_____

_____

_____

6. What can we learn from their prayer that would encourage us to be a fellowship devoted to outreach—even against strong opposition?

_____

_____

_____

_____

_____

7. How is their prayer answered (v 31)?

_____

_____

_____

_____

Apply

FOR YOURSELF: Am I devoted to my church—its teaching, fellowship, mission, mutual care and generosity? Are there areas of church life where I am basically selfish, looking for what I can get out of it rather than what I can give to it?

_____

_____

_____

FOR YOUR CHURCH: How can we as a fellowship grow to be more like the picture of a "missionary family" that we see in these passages? Think of some practical steps you might take together.

_____

_____

_____

_____

Pray

Spend some time thanking God for the way he has drawn you into the fellowship of your church with one another, and for what he is doing through you in the world.

FOR THE GROUP: Share the names of two people you know who you would like an opportunity to share the gospel with—a family member, a friend at work or a neighbor. Pray very specifically for boldness to talk with them about Christ.

FOR YOUR WHOLE CHURCH: Pray that you would encourage each other to be a "missionary family" week by week. And that you would grow together as a generous, loving, attractive family.

SERMON NOTES

Bible passage: Date:

_____

_____

_____

_____

_____

_____

_____

_____

_____

_____

_____

_____

_____

_____

_____

_____

_____

_____

_____

_____

_____

_____

SESSION 4:

WHO ARE WE REACHING?

IF WE ARE TO BE EFFECTIVE WITNESSES FOR CHRIST,
THEN WE NEED TO KNOW NOT ONLY ABOUT HIM, AND
ABOUT OURSELVES, BUT ABOUT THE PEOPLE WE LONG
TO TALK TO ABOUT HIM. IN THIS SESSION, WE SHALL
DISCOVER HOW JESUS SAW THOSE AROUND HIM, AND
CONSIDER HOW THAT SHOULD SHAPE OUR ATTITUDES
AND ACTIONS AS HIS PEOPLE.

WHO ARE WE REACHING?

Discuss

What are some of the different labels we give to people who are not Christians?

_____

_____

_____

_____

How do these affect how we view them and relate to them?

_____

_____

_____

_____

_____

▶ **WATCH DVD 4.1 OR LISTEN TO TALK 4.1**

_____

_____

_____

_____

_____

_____

_____

63

Discuss

Without Christ, people are dead in their sins, walking in the way of the world and enslaved to the evil one (see Ephesians 2:1-3).

Why do we find it difficult to see people in the way the Bible describes them?

How can we help ourselves to see unbelievers through God's eyes?

Christians can be condescending toward unbelievers, or apathetic about their condition. Which of these attitudes do you think you are more likely to fall into, and why?

What happens when a church as a whole exhibits one or other of these traits, or both?

_____

_____

_____

_____

What is the solution to these ungodly attitudes?

_____

_____

_____

_____

▶ **WATCH DVD 4.2 OR LISTEN TO TALK 4.2**

_____

_____

_____

_____

_____

_____

_____

_____

_____

_____

_____

_____

_____

_____

Discuss

 **MATTHEW 9:35-38**

> ³⁵ And Jesus went throughout all the cities and villages, teaching in their synagogues and proclaiming the gospel of the kingdom and healing every disease and every affliction. ³⁶ When he saw the crowds, he had compassion for them, because they were harassed and helpless, like sheep without a shepherd. ³⁷ Then he said to his disciples, "The harvest is plentiful, but the laborers are few; ³⁸ therefore pray earnestly to the Lord of the harvest to send out laborers into his harvest."

What drives Jesus' compassion for people?

_____

_____

_____

_____

"Harassed," "helpless," "sheep without a shepherd." Can you see how this is a good description for your friends and neighbors who are not Christians?

_____

_____

_____

_____

_____

In the passage above, what does Jesus' love for the people cause him to do?

_____

_____

_____

Are you tempted to think that some people are "beyond" the gospel message for any reason? Why is that thinking so wrong?

_____

_____

_____

_____

When you first visited church, what was familiar to you? What was strange? What are you doing now to make visitors welcome, and your meetings understandable—whether or not they believe in Jesus?

_____

_____

Pray

Ask God to forgive you for times when you have failed to show true compassion to unbelievers; for example, through apathy, condescension or thinking they are beyond saving.

In Session 1 you were asked to think of two people you would like to share the gospel with this month (see page 18). Ask God to help you truly see these people in the way he sees them—as "harassed and helpless, like sheep without a shepherd."

Pray that you will see others more and more through biblical eyes, and that this will motivate you to tell them about Jesus.

DAILY BIBLE DEVOTIONALS

People around us are hungry and hurting, just as in Jesus' day. So we need to learn to have the compassion of Christ, which we'll witness each day this week.

Day 1

MARK 5:21-34

This woman's bleeding (v 25) was not only inconvenient and expensive; it was excluding. This condition would have made her an outcast from the temple, the synagogues and society (read Leviticus 15:25-31). Her situation was hopeless.

Q: *So why do you think she is "trembling" as she admits to Jesus that she touched him (v 33)?*

But Jesus does not recoil from her touch. He replaces her hopelessness with peace (v 34). He gives her freedom to be herself, to look forward. In essence, he gives her back her life.

Q: *Where is Jesus heading (v 22-24)? How do we see his compassion in stopping for this woman?*

Q: *Who are the people in your society in a similar position to this woman? Do you feel compassion toward them? How might you touch them with the gospel of hope?*

PRAY: *Lord, thank you that you had time for outcasts, and brought peace to them. Please give me your compassion.*

Day 2

LUKE 19:1-10

Tax collectors worked for the Romans, growing rich by overcharging on taxes. They were hated as traitors. Zacchaeus has traded in his reputation and morals to get rich. And he has what he wants (v 2).

Q: *But how do verses 3-4 suggest he hasn't found what he seeks in wealth?*

Jesus could have visited with anyone in that town. He chose Zacchaeus (v 5).

Q: *What does his decision do to his reputation with others (v 7)?*

To offer compassion, Jesus had to risk his reputation. Soon, he would need to give up his life. Those who have much but are still hungry can find what they seek as they invite Jesus in as Lord of their lives and let go of what they once worshiped (v 8).

Q: *Who are the people you know who are similar to Zacchaeus? How can you show compassion to them?*

PRAY: *Please lead me to those who are rich, but are still hungry. Please give me your compassion.*

Day 3

JOHN 3:1-15

Q: *Who is Nicodemus (v 1)?*

But beneath Nicodemus' exalted position lies confusion. Why else would this insider, this religious leader, feel the need to visit Jesus under cover of darkness (v 2)?

Q: *What does Jesus tell him is the way into God's eternal kingdom (v 3, 5)?*

We can do many things; but none of us can give birth to ourselves. Jesus is saying: *You may have achieved many things, but you cannot bring yourself into God's kingdom. That is like being born—it is not your initiative, nor your achievement.*

Jesus shows that compassion can be combined with conviction. He gently points out that Nicodemus does not know as much as everyone thinks he does (v 10). He firmly explains to this Pharisee that he will never find the answers he seeks in his own religious system. He clearly points this successful man to the truth that it is belief in him that leads to life (v 15). And wonderfully, Nicodemus listened and, at last, understood (read John 19:38-42).

Q: *Who are the people in your community who are like Nicodemus? How can you show compassion to them?*

PRAY: *Thank you that you gave clarity to the confused and pointed the elite to the cross. Please give me your compassion.*

Day 4

The desire to be loved is intrinsic to being human. Where do we seek what we need?

JOHN 4:1-30

Safety, climate and propriety meant women went to the well in a group, in the evening. In verse 7 we meet a woman, alone, in the heat of the day. *And Jesus speaks to her.*

Q: *What does he ask for, and what does he offer (v 7, 10, 13-14)?*

Q: *To what issue does Jesus take the conversation next (v 16-18)?*

This woman has been looking for living water in the wrong place—and she has returned to that poisoned well six times. No human relationship can give us what only God can; it will break under the strain of that demand. In our century more than any other, people have been hurt and kept hungry by the lie that in human relationships, we find all the love we need. Jesus does not condemn her; rather, he offers her living, lasting water—himself.

Q: *What does she discover is different about this man (v 19, 25-26, 29)?*

Q: *Who are the people similar to this woman near you? How can you show compassion to them?*

PRAY: *Lord, help me not to judge those looking for love in the wrong places. Please give me your compassion.*

Day 5

LUKE 7:36-50

Q: *How does the sinful woman—the implication is she is a prostitute—treat Jesus (v 37-38)? How does Jesus compare this with how the religious leader, Simon, treats him (v 44-46)?*

Q: *How does Simon appear to think Jesus should treat this woman (v 39)? How does Jesus treat her (v 48, 50)?*

The gospel is not offensive to the broken, but to the "good." Jesus will never make sense to us until we look at him through our tears over our sin. Not only are hurt and hunger not *obstacles* to coming to Jesus—they are *prerequisites*. The hurting and hungry are closer to grasping the gospel than the sorted and proud, as Jesus points out in his parable in verses 41-42.

The challenge for those of us who claim the name of Jesus is: *which man at the table are you like?* In your home, would a woman such as this be made welcome, and told about Jesus? In your church, who are there more of—broken sinners who cry over their flaws, or upstanding people who see no need to cry at all?

Q: *Who are the people in your area who are like this woman? How can you show compassion to them?*

PRAY: *Lord, I know I am a sinner, saved by you. Make me more like you than the Pharisee. Give me your compassion.*

Day 6

Q: *Why do you think many people hear of Jesus' compassion and offer of eternal life, and walk away from them?*

MARK 10:17-31

Q: *What is this man worried about (v 17)?*

If there is any question that should keep people awake at night, this is it. And if eternity could be earned by rule-keeping, this man would be doing great (v 19-20).

Q: *How does Jesus feel about him (v 21)?*

Q: *What "one thing" is lacking from this man's life (end of v 21)?*

Jesus is saying: *If you want eternal life, you must do nothing and you must give everything. Put me first and be willing to give anything for me, and I will give you what your wealth will not buy you and your works will not merit you.*

Jesus does not dismiss this man; neither does he pander to him. He would rather the man walked away than follow under false pretenses. Compassion does not compromise; love tells the truth, and risks rejection. And in the end, this man decides to choose his wealth over his eternity (v 22).

Q: *Who do you know like this? How can you show compassion to them?*

PRAY: *Thank you for lovingly not compromising. Please give me your compassion.*

 # JOURNAL

What I've learned or been particularly struck by this week...

_____

_____

_____

_____

_____

What I want to change in my perspectives or actions as a result of this week...

_____

_____

_____

_____

_____

Things I would like to think about more or discuss with others at my church...

_____

_____

_____

_____

_____

BIBLE STUDY

Discuss

Think about a major change that you have undergone in your life—from single to married; from study to work; from living with parents to living independently, etc. What were some of the big things you loved about your "new life"? What were some of the things you were previously concerned about that disappeared?

☛ READ EPHESIANS 2:1-10

> ¹ *And you were dead in the trespasses and sins…*

1. What three things do people who are not Christians follow, according to Paul?

_____

_____

2. What phrases describe the consequences of this way of thinking and living for the present (v 1), and the future (v 3)? What do these phrases actually mean?

_____

_____

Why is there no excuse for "walking" in sin?

_____

_____

3. What does this way of living look like in the reality of people's daily lives?

_____

_____

_____

Think back to before you were a Christian. In what ways can you now see that verses 1-3 were true of you?

_____

_____

How would you have responded back then to being described in this way?

_____

_____

4. What three words does Paul use in verses 4-5 to describe the character of God? Explain what they mean from the passage.

_____

_____

5. What three big things does God do for those he saves (v 5, 6, 10)? How should we feel about these?

_____

_____

6. How are people saved, and how are they not saved (v 8-9)?

_____

_____

How is it possible to be very religious and very spiritually dead?

_____

_____

7. How might remembering both how we were without Christ and what Christ has done for us help us as we speak to others about the gospel?

_____

_____

Apply

FOR YOURSELF: It is easy to see people in general as an inconvenience, a way of getting what you want, or a way of making you happy or contented. What would change if you always saw unbelievers as hopeless and helpless sinners, who need to experience the love of God in Christ?

FOR YOUR CHURCH: How would it help your church if they remembered and applied the following truths?

● We were dead in sins (v 1).

● People are by nature children of wrath (v 3).

● We have been saved by grace (v 8).

● No one may boast (v 9).

Pray

Talk about the people you prayed together for last week. Have there been any opportunities with them this week? Continue to pray for them.

FOR YOURSELF: Ask God to help you see others as he sees them. Ask that God would fill you with love and compassion for them.

FOR YOUR WHOLE CHURCH: Ask the Lord to help your church be loving toward those who are not yet Christians. Pray that outsiders will see the love, mercy and grace of God modeled in your life together.

 # SERMON NOTES

Bible passage: Date:

SESSION 5:

WHAT IS THE GOSPEL PLAN?

THE GOSPEL IS ALL ABOUT THE LIFE, DEATH, RESURRECTION AND RULE OF JESUS, GOD THE SON. AND THIS GOSPEL IS GOD THE FATHER'S INITIATIVE – HE SENT HIS SON TO BE HIS PEOPLE'S LORD AND SAVIOR. SO WHEN DID THIS PLAN BEGIN? WHERE IS IT ALL HEADING? AND HOW DOES THAT CHANGE HOW WE VIEW OUR ROLE AS GOSPEL WITNESSES?

WHAT IS THE GOSPEL PLAN?

GENESIS
THE BOOK OF
BEGINNINGS

REVELATION
THE BOOK
OF ENDINGS

CREATION

FALL

PROMISE

▶ **WATCH DVD 5.1 OR LISTEN TO TALK 5.1**

Discuss

"The fall had both vertical and horizontal consequences." What evidence is there in your neighborhood that these consequences are still being experienced today?

👉 **GENESIS 3:15**

[The Lᴏʀᴅ God said to the serpent:] *"I will put enmity between you and the woman, and between your offspring and her offspring; he shall bruise your head, and you shall bruise his heel."*

The gospel was God's plan right from the very beginning. What can we see from the promise in Genesis 3:15 about the "who, what and how" of salvation?

_____

_____

_____

_____

_____

_____

GENESIS
THE BOOK OF BEGINNINGS

REVELATION
THE BOOK OF ENDINGS

CREATION   FALL   PROMISE   RETURN   JUDGMENT   NEW CREATION

▶ **WATCH DVD 5.2 OR LISTEN TO TALK 5.2**

_____

_____

_____

_____

_____

(lines for notes)

Discuss

☞ **REVELATION 5:5-6**

> [5] And one of the elders said to me, "Weep no more; behold, the Lion of the tribe of Judah, the Root of David, has conquered, so that he can open the scroll and its seven seals." [6] And between the throne and the four living creatures and among the elders I saw a Lamb standing, as though it had been slain...

How do the descriptions of Jesus in this passage show us that God's gospel plan has been unfolding throughout history?

The end of God's gospel plan is to gather his redeemed people in the new creation to worship the Lord forever. How should this prospect motivate us for evangelism now?

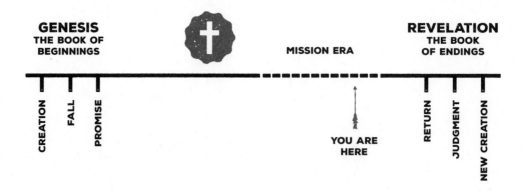

▶ WATCH DVD 5.3 OR LISTEN TO TALK 5.3

_____

_____

_____

_____

_____

👉 MATTHEW 28:18-20

¹⁸ "All authority in heaven and on earth has been given to me. ¹⁹ Go therefore and make disciples of all nations, baptizing them in the name of the Father and of the Son and of the Holy Spirit, ²⁰ teaching them to observe all that I have commanded you. And behold, I am with you always, to the end of the age."

What is our specific job in the "mission era" (see diagram above)?

_____

_____

_____

_____

When does our job finish?

_____

_____

_____

_____

_____

"We are not the chef, cooking up the gospel meal; we are simply the waiter, delivering the food to the table."

The gospel plan is God's work that we are privileged to be involved in. How does this liberate us from both inaction and fear?

_____

_____

_____

_____

_____

_____

Pray

"Worthy is the Lamb who was slain, to receive power and wealth and wisdom and might and honor and glory and blessing!" Use these words from Revelation 5:12 to thank and praise Jesus.

DAILY BIBLE DEVOTIONALS

The gospel of Jesus Christ has always been God's plan. Throughout the Old Testament, he gave his people glimpses of it. This week, we'll enjoy six of them.

Day 1

God's promises to Abraham—a people, a land, and his blessing—all rested on his son, Isaac. But then God asked Abraham something almost incomprehensible.

GENESIS 22:1-19

Q: *What must Abraham do (v 2)? Where?*

Q: *Why does Isaac not die (v 11-14)?*

Q: *Read John 3:16. What similarities do you see between what Abraham was willing to do, and what God did do?*

God did not ask Abraham to do anything he himself would not do. Isaac was laid on a wooden altar; God's Son was laid on a wooden cross. But there was no stand-in for Jesus. He *was* the stand-in. God sacrificed his only Son, not out of obedience but out of love.

And where did God do this? Jerusalem, a city built on a mountain which centuries before had a different name: Mount Moriah. As Abraham prepared to give his only son, we see a shadow of God's gospel plan that should greatly thrill us and deeply move us.

PRAY: *Turn John 3:16 into a prayer of praise and deep gratitude to God.*

Day 2

Abraham's descendants multiplied, but they became slaves in Egypt. God freed them—but now they face Pharaoh's army.

EXODUS 14:5-31

The Israelites are utterly terrified (v 10).

Q: *What does Moses tell the people to do, and promise God will do (v 14)?*

Q: *How does God fight for his people and win (v 15-18, 21-29)?*

The people learned on the two shores of the Red Sea: *don't be scared—God wins.* He rescued his people by crushing his enemies through the work of his servant.
But we face a far worse enemy than Pharaoh—implacable, invincible death.

Q: *Read Romans 6:8-9. How did God fight death for his people and win?*

How do we respond to the death of death? Like Israel to the death of Pharaoh's army (Exodus 14:31)—with awed respect for God and a total trust in his rescuing Servant, Jesus.

PRAY: *Use Exodus 14:31 to guide your response to God right now.*

Day 3

With Egypt behind them, God's people traveled to God's land. But one of their worst enemies went with them—themselves.

READ NUMBERS 21:4-9

Q: *What do the people complain about?*

This "worthless" food is the manna God had miraculously provided (Exodus 16). The people are effectively saying: *We don't want to live with and rely on you in this world.* In sending the serpents, God says: *OK, you won't.* Poisonous snakes were normal in the desert; miraculous food was not. The people have chosen life without God, complete with suffering and death.

Q: *Who provides the solution. How (v 8-9)?*

Israel lived (v 9); but this must have seemed a strange way for God to offer healing!

Q: *Read John 3:14-15. What was God pointing to in this wilderness incident?*

God's plan has always been to rescue people from the consequences of their own choices. He did it through a bronze snake when his people were facing certain death; he has done it eternally through the Lord Jesus when we were facing certain hell. We, like they, need only look at the One who is lifted up, and trust him to heal us.

PRAY: *Use Numbers 21:7 to confess your sin to God and thank him for his mercy.*

Day 4

In Genesis 3:15, God promised that a man would come who would defeat the serpent (Satan) at his strongest moment.

1 SAMUEL 17:1-11, 32-54

God's people lived in God's land, but were threatened by the Philistines. Israel chose a king, Saul—but God had rejected him and had chosen a new one, the boy David.

Q: *How do Saul and David react very differently to Goliath (v 11, 32, 37)?*

In describing Goliath, "coat of mail" (v 5) is literally simply "scales." Here is an enemy of God's people, covered in scales. Goliath is the serpent—and he is very strong.

Q: *What does God's chosen king do (v 48-49)? How, and how not (v 50)?*

Here is how God works—he defeats the great serpent through his chosen king. Here we get a glimpse of God's ultimate Warrior-King, Jesus, defeating the devil. And just as David did not use the weapons of worldly kings, so Jesus would use the most surprising weapon of all to render Satan powerless: his blood. At the moment the devil seemed strongest— the death of the Son of God—he was utterly defeated. So we are not David, fighting and winning. We are the Israelites: powerless, yet victorious, watching our King fight and win.

PRAY: *Read Revelation 19:11-16. Praise Jesus, your victorious Warrior-King.*

Day 5

After David and his son Solomon, the kings of God's people did not seek to obey God, and so forfeited God's blessing and peace.

2 KINGS 5:1-19A

Q: *What is great about Naaman (v 1)? But… what is not great (v 1)?*

Not only was leprosy an incurable disease that often led to death; it was a sign of spiritual uncleanness that always led to exclusion from God's presence (see Numbers 5:1-3).

Q: *How does Naaman hear about God's prophet, and from whom (v 2-5)? How does this encourage you to witness?*

Q: *Naaman is told how he can be healed (v 10). Why does he very nearly end up not healed (v 11-13)?*

Many people's problem with the gospel is its simplicity! God says: *Trust a man dying on a cross, and you will enjoy perfect life in my presence eternally.* And we think: *Is that it? Surely I have to do something.* It is hard to believe God has done everything, and all we have to do is let him wash us. Peter had the same problem as Naaman—**read John 13:3-9.** We, like they, need to accept what is written on each page of the word of God: *You will not enter God's presence by what you do, but by what God has done.*

PRAY: *Use John 13:8-9 to admit your need of Jesus' work and thank him for it.*

Day 6

God's people were now in exile, many in Persia. One, Esther, Mordecai's cousin, was queen. But the king's minister, Haman, convinced the king to have all Jews killed.

ESTHER 4:10 - 5:5; 7:2-10

Q: *What is Esther willing to risk in order to speak to the king uninvited (4:11, 16)?*

As Esther bravely approaches the king, he invites her to speak (5:2). So she invites him and Haman to a series of feasts. At the second feast, Esther reveals the plot to the king, pleads for the lives of her people, and identifies the ringleader (7:3-6).

Q: *How does the king respond (v 9-10)?*

Q: *Mordecai had suggested Esther had "come to the kingdom for such a time as this" (4:14). How was he right?*

A member of the royal family risks her life so that she can speak to the all-powerful king and save her people. Esther gives us a glimpse of Jesus, a member of creation's royal family. He did not merely risk death, but tasted death, so that he can rescue us from the wrath of the King and keep us safe from our enemies. But unlike the king of Persia, the King of creation was the initiator of the plan—the plan to send Jesus when the time was exactly right in order to die for his people. **Read Romans 5:6-8.**

PRAY: *Use Romans 5:6-8 to thank God for his plan, and Jesus for his sacrifice.*

JOURNAL

What I've learned or been particularly struck by this week…

_____

_____

_____

_____

_____

_____

What I want to change in my perspectives or actions as a result of this week…

_____

_____

_____

_____

_____

_____

Things I would like to think about more or discuss with others at my church…

_____

_____

_____

_____

_____

Discuss

Have you ever been involved in organizing something where it has not been clear who has been in charge and what specific roles people were playing? What happened? What lessons were learned?

☞ READ ACTS 16:11-34

1. What evangelistic strategy did Paul and Silas have (v 13)? In what other ways and in what other places did God use them while they were in Philippi (v 16-18, 23-30)?

2. What kinds of people became the first Christians in Philippi? Can you think of modern parallels to the different kinds of people that responded to the gospel?

3. What was the order of events in the conversion of Lydia? Who did what?

4. What happens to our witness if we forget that:

- it is God's work to open people's hearts and minds to the gospel?

_____

_____

- God does his work as his people open their mouths and proclaim the gospel?

_____

_____

5. So what counts as success in evangelism? What counts as failure?

_____

_____

How does this understanding of both God's part and our part in outreach liberate us to be more active and bold in evangelism?

_____

_____

6. What are the biggest reasons why we don't share the gospel more with other people?

_____

_____

How does the experience of Paul and Silas in evangelism in this passage help us with these? Try to give specific examples of how this might work in your life.

_____

_____

_____

_____

7. Imagine going to a meeting of the church in Philippi shortly after the events in this chapter. Who would be in the congregation? What kinds of unbelievers might also have been present? How does this showcase God's gospel plan?

    How might remembering God's gospel plan to call all kinds of people change the way we think about outreach?

Apply

FOR YOURSELF: What difference will knowing both your part and God's part in evangelism make to you this week?

FOR YOUR CHURCH: To what extent are you genuinely showing in your congregation that God's gospel plan is to call people from every nation and every stratum of society? What can you do differently to make sure you are not unhelpfully discriminating in your outreach?

Pray

Think about the two people you have been praying for. And then pray that God would do his work of opening their hearts as you speak the gospel.

FOR YOURSELF: Pray that you would understand that God calls us just to speak, and that you would rejoice in the work God is doing in the world.

FOR YOUR WHOLE CHURCH: Pray that you would grow in boldness to reach out with the gospel to everyone and anyone.

SERMON NOTES

Bible passage: Date:

SESSION 6:

HOW SHOULD WE PRAY?

"EFFECTIVE EVANGELISM BEGINS WITH PERSEVERING PRAYER," WROTE THE ENGLISH PASTOR DICK LUCAS. WE MUST REACH UP TO GOD IF WE ARE TO REACH OUT TO PEOPLE. IN THIS SESSION, WE WILL CONSIDER WHY PRAYER IS SO VITAL, AND WHAT THE CONTENT OF OUR PRAYING ABOUT WITNESS SHOULD BE.

HOW SHOULD WE PRAY?

Discuss

Have you ever prayed for an opportunity to talk about Jesus to someone? What happened?

_____

_____

_____

_____

_____

_____

▶ WATCH DVD 6.1 OR LISTEN TO TALK 6.1

_____

_____

_____

_____

_____

_____

_____

_____

_____

_____

_____

Discuss

 **MATTHEW 9:37-38**

> ³⁷ *Then he said to his disciples, "The harvest is plentiful, but the laborers are few;* ³⁸ *therefore pray earnestly to the Lord of the harvest to send out laborers into his harvest."*

Erik said: *"We tend to think that the harvest is puny and the workers abound."* Why do we think this?

_____

_____

_____

_____

What would change for us if we really believed the opposite?

_____

_____

_____

_____

_____

"The human heart is a formidable mountain, unable to be opened by any amount of human exertion." How is this both a challenge and an encouragement to us?

_____

_____

_____

_____

Pray

"Prayer connects us with the unlimited resources of our Father in heaven."

Thank God that there is a ripe harvest, and pray for workers to go into the harvest field of:

- your family
- your neighborhood
- your workplace

Pray that your church will be a missionary family that is reaching out to the area it is situated in.

"Lord, give me an opportunity to tell some else about the gospel today—and please don't be subtle!" Why not pray this prayer for each other now?

▶ **WATCH DVD 6.2 OR LISTEN TO TALK 6.2**

Discuss

👉 **EPHESIANS 6:18-20**

18 ... making supplication for all the saints, 19 and also for me, that words may be given to me in opening my mouth boldly to proclaim the mystery of the gospel, 20 for which I am an ambassador in chains, that I may declare it boldly, as I ought to speak.

In Session 1, we saw from this passage that Paul asked people to pray for words and for boldness. Have you been praying for boldness for yourself and others? If you have, what has happened? If you haven't, why not?

_____

_____

_____

_____

_____

"Imagine what would happen in your life, your church family and your city if you and other believers started praying like a missionary."
What do you imagine might happen?

_____

_____

_____

_____

_____

_____

_____

What practical changes can you make so that you don't just *imagine* praying like a missionary, but it begins to happen in reality?

_____

_____

_____

_____

_____

_____

Pray

Spend some time in prayer for each other and your church as a whole:

- Pray for faithfulness.
- Pray for boldness.
- Pray for blessing.

DAILY BIBLE DEVOTIONALS

Prayer is the fuel of evangelism. This week we focus on Colossians 4; on Paul's instructions for prayer and the lifestyle that flows from a biblical prayer life.

Day 1

COLOSSIANS 4:2

Q: *What three hallmarks of prayer does Paul command us to display?*

Prayer is not always easy. It often takes effort to get to your knees. Paul spoke of one of his friends, Epaphras, "struggling" or "wrestling" (v 12) in prayer. Prayer is a discipline; we need to be "steadfast."

What will help us? Becoming "watchful." Watch out for what to pray for; and then watch out for your prayers being answered. The first will give content to your prayers; the second, motivation. As you listen to your friends (Christians and non-believers) speak, ask: *How can I be praying for them?*

As we learn to notice God answering prayers, we will be full of "thanksgiving." Each day's prayers will begin with gratitude for the answers to yesterday's! Prayer and praise grow hand in hand.

Q: *How will you exhibit more steadfastness, watchfulness and thanksgiving in your own prayer life?*

PRAY: *Pray that you will pray like this. Ask for each of these three hallmarks.*

Day 2

COLOSSIANS 4:3

Q: *Who does Paul ask for prayer for?*

However distant our friends, and however difficult their circumstances, we are never powerless because we can always pray. If even an apostle needed prayer, every Christian does—including you and me.

Q: *What does Paul ask for prayer for?*

The "mystery" is "Christ in you, the hope of glory" (1:27). This is the gospel: the King lives in us now, and we will live with the King in glory in eternity. We need to ask God to open the doors for that message; and then we need to ask God to enable us to walk through those doors and "declare" that message. If you feel you don't get many open doors for the gospel, consider these questions: *Am I actually asking for open doors? Am I looking for them? And am I ready to walk through them?*

Q: *Whose witness will you steadfastly pray for? Who can you ask to be steadfast in praying for yours?*

PRAY: *Pray Paul's prayer request for a couple of Christian friends right now.*

Day 3

COLOSSIANS 4:3

Q: *Where is Paul writing these words?*

Q: *What, does he suggest, is the cause of him being there?*

Q: *If you were where Paul was, what would naturally be your top prayer request?*

The only door most of us would want to open would be the cell door—but not Paul! He cares more about witnessing than freedom, and so he most wants to share the word of the gospel, rather than to walk free from jail.

Being a suffering person does not mean exemption from being a witnessing believer. Our circumstances must never be used as an excuse for not evangelizing. Rather, our circumstances can always be opportunities for witnessing. Here, the apostle sees his prison as a mission field. A man I know was hospitalized for months in his thirties, and started a Bible study in his hospital ward. We are to have the same priority. Of course we may pray for our circumstances to be changed; but we must also be praying for our circumstances to be used.

Q: *Does this challenge you right now? Do you ever use your circumstances as a reason for not witnessing faithfully?*

PRAY: *Confess anything you need to. Ask for Paul's heart so that you pray his prayer.*

Day 4

COLOSSIANS 4:4

Q: *What does Paul pray about how he declares the gospel?*

Q: *Have you had ever failed to explain the gospel this way?*

Clarity is a necessity in gospel proclamation. How can we fail to be clear? We can obscure the gospel by a non-declaration of crucial parts of the gospel message; this may avoid offending someone but it also obscures the glory of the gospel. But equally, we can be unclear through over-complication—if we seek to give an exhaustive explanation, we give no explanation at all!

Elsewhere, the Scriptures tell us to make sure we are "prepared" for declaring the gospel (1 Peter 3:15). But Paul here shows us that clarity is a supernatural gift. He wanted *prayer* for clarity; it is a prayer we should pray for ourselves and others. We should ask God to give us the words that mean we walk away from a gospel opportunity not only knowing that we took it, but that we took it *well*. We should pray that, under God's direction, our words will be exactly what is needed for the gospel to resonate with the person we are speaking to, impacting not only their heads but their hearts in a way that makes sense to them and is attractive to them.

PRAY: *Pray for clarity, and against non-declaration and over-complication.*

Day 5

COLOSSIANS 4:5

Verses 5-6 make clear that sharing the gospel is a task for all believers; so Paul's prayer in verses 3-4 should be ours, too.

Q: *Yet verse 5 is nothing to do with what we say! What is the focus here?*

Q: *What happens to our evangelistic opportunities and conversations if we are not obeying verse 5, do you think?*

Time is short—Jesus' return is certain, but we do not know its schedule. We must "[make] the best use" of each day until that Day, by showing those around us that there is another, more satisfying and more hope-filled way to walk through life.

In order to be able to talk the gospel, we must first walk the gospel—and we must walk it in clear view of those who do not yet know Jesus as Lord. "Outsiders" need to see the difference that "Christ in you, the hope of glory" makes to real people's real lives. Our conduct will either undergird or undermine our evangelistic efforts.

Q: *Are you sharing life with those who do not know Jesus? Do you need to use your time differently?*

Q: *How well is your life promoting the gospel? How can it do so more?*

PRAY: *Ask for divine help to see how you can walk more wisely each day.*

Day 6

COLOSSIANS 4:6

Paul cares about what we say when we are having a "gospel conversation." But he tells us also to be concerned with what we say about the gospel when we are having an "ordinary conversation."

Q: *Grace is a good one-word summary both of the character of God and the content of the gospel. So what is "gracious" conversation, do you think?*

Q: *Consider how salt changes a meal. What does it mean for our words to be "seasoned with salt," do you think?*

If the content of our everyday conversations do not ever mention the gospel, or the tone of those interactions do not reflect the gracious, generous, forgiving character of God, we should not be surprised if no one ever asks us about the gospel of God! This does not call for blandness—quite the opposite. A Christian's ordinary conversation is salty: scattered with distinctive, attractive grains of gospel truth. These kinds of interactions, allied to a distinctive life (v 5), are what lead to questions being asked—and to gospel-filled answers that sound honest and real.

Q: *Reflect on your ordinary interactions. How can they be more flavored with God's gospel, in content and tone?*

PRAY: *Ask God to grow you in grace-filled saltiness in your conversations.*

 **JOURNAL**

What I've learned or been particularly struck by this week…

_____

_____

_____

_____

_____

_____

What I want to change in my perspectives or actions as a result of this week…

_____

_____

_____

_____

_____

_____

Things I would like to think about more or discuss with others at my church…

_____

_____

_____

_____

_____

BIBLE STUDY

Discuss

Think back to when you were a child. What particular things did you do that particularly pleased your parents or teachers? Why were they pleased with these things? What effect did that have on you?

👉 READ 1 TIMOTHY 2:1-7

> [1] *First of all, then, I urge that supplications, prayers, intercessions, and thanksgivings be made for all people…*

1. What, does Paul tell us, pleases God (v 1-3)? What does God desire (v 4)?

_____

_____

_____

_____

2. Who are we to pray for?

_____

_____

_____

What is the purpose of praying for all those "in high positions" (v 2, 4)?

_____

_____

_____

3. How is God described in these verses? How does this help us see the priority of evangelism for Christians and churches?

_____

_____

_____

4. What are some of the reasons why we fail to pray for the gospel to advance?

_____

_____

_____

How do these truths about God encourage us to pray?

_____

_____

_____

5. How is Christ described in verses 5-6? How does that help us with the content of what our message should be?

_____

_____

_____

_____

_____

6. How do these truths about Jesus encourage us to pray?

_____

_____

_____

Apply

FOR YOURSELF: Who do you find it hardest to pray for and why? How can you help yourself to be more consistent and persistent with your prayers for others to find Christ?

_____

_____

_____

FOR YOUR GROUP: How can you encourage each other to pray, not just for health problems or other life difficulties, but also for more proactive evangelism?

_____

_____

_____

FOR YOUR CHURCH: What opportunities are there for you to pray together for your outreach as a whole church? How can you keep prayer for outreach high up the agenda?

_____

_____

_____

Pray

Pray again for the people you requested prayer for last week. Share any news for thanksgiving and encouragement. How has God answered your prayers from last week?

FOR YOUR WHOLE CHURCH: Pray that you would become a church dedicated to praying to the Lord of the harvest for him to work through you to bring "all people" under the sound of the only gospel that can save them.

SERMON NOTES

Bible passage: Date:

SESSION 7:
WHAT DO WE SAY?

IF WE ARE PRAYING FOR OPPORTUNITIES AND LOOKING FOR OPPORTUNITIES TO SHARE THE GOSPEL, THEN WE WILL FIND OURSELVES IN POSITIONS WHERE WE ARE ABLE TO TALK ABOUT THE GOSPEL. BUT... WHAT DO WE ACTUALLY SAY? WHAT ARE THE THINGS WE MUST AIM TO TALK ABOUT, AND HOW DO WE SPEAK ABOUT THE GOSPEL IN WAYS THAT MAKE SENSE AND RESONATE WITH THOSE WE'RE SPEAKING TO? THOSE ARE THE QUESTIONS WE WILL CONSIDER IN THE NEXT TWO SESSIONS.

WHAT DO WE SAY?

Discuss

Have you ever learned or used a gospel outline (The Bridge to Life, The Roman Road, The Wordless Book, Two Ways to Live, etc.)? What do you think was good about it? Was there anything that was not so good?

▶ WATCH DVD 7.1 OR LISTEN TO TALK 7.1

- *In this session, we're thinking about how we explain the gospel to others. As you watch the DVD or listen to the talk, make a note of any phrases or ideas that you personally might find helpful when sharing the gospel.*

1 CORINTHIANS 15:1-8

¹ Now I would remind you, brothers, of the gospel I preached to you, which you received, in which you stand, ² and by which you are being saved, if you hold fast to the word I preached to you—unless you believed in vain.

³ For I delivered to you as of first importance what I also received: that Christ died for our sins in accordance with the Scriptures, ⁴ that he was buried, that he was raised on the third day in accordance with the Scriptures, ⁵ and that he appeared to Cephas, then to the twelve. ⁶ Then he appeared to more than five hundred brothers at one time, most of whom are still alive, though some have fallen asleep. ⁷ Then he appeared to James, then to all the apostles. ⁸ Last of all, as to one untimely born, he appeared also to me.

Discuss

In 1 Corinthians 15, Paul is reminding the Christians in Corinth about the message he shared with them. What does he tell us about the gospel in verses 1 and 2?

The word "gospel" means "good news." The gospel message is the good news about Jesus. Underline the things we learn about Jesus in verses 3-8.

Paul says that delivering the message about Jesus is "of first importance" (v 3).
How would you tell someone the good news about Jesus in just one minute? Use
the words and phrases you underlined to help you.

What do you think people would find weird from your explanation?

Would they have found anything offensive?

How might you start to unpack some of those weird or offensive ideas in a way that is helpful for them?

Life does not always offer us an opportunity to say everything about the gospel. What advantages and pitfalls are there in communicating only part of the gospel message in a conversation?

_____

_____

_____

_____

_____

Set aside some time this week to practice your quick explanation of the gospel. When will you do that?

_____

_____

_____

Pray

Look again at the words and phrases you underlined in verses 3-8. Thank and praise Jesus for each of these truths about him.

Ask God to help you refine your explanation of the gospel as you practice it this week.

Continue to pray for the people you want to share the gospel with.

DAILY BIBLE DEVOTIONALS

The content of the gospel never changes; but the context always does. This week, we'll see different ways Jesus and his apostles explained the gospel.

Day 1

The gospel consists of three elements:
• the *person* of Jesus (who he is);
• the *purpose* of Jesus (why he came);
• and the *summons* of Jesus (how we respond).

MARK 1:14-15

These are the first words of Jesus that Mark records in his Gospel. "The kingdom of God is at hand" is Jesus' way of explaining both who he is (the King, come near) and why he has come (to invite people into his kingdom by opening the way into his kingdom, through his death and resurrection). Notice that Jesus is pointing people to the Old Testament to understand his person and purpose. In this "time" of history, God's promises are "fulfilled," as "the kingdom"—the perfect reign of God's eternal King—comes to earth.

Q: *What does Jesus summon people to do (v 15)?*

We could sum this up as: *turn and trust.*

Q: *If you had a minute to explain the gospel, how could you use verse 15?*

PRAY: *Spend time thanking Jesus for the good news laid out in these verses.*

Day 2

LUKE 9:18-26

Q: *How does Jesus tell his disciples in verses 18-22 about: (a) his person; (b) his summons?*

Jesus' purpose centers on his death and resurrection (v 22). We must speak of both.

Q: *How does Jesus outline his summons in verses 23-26? Is this the way you / your church frame the summons?*

It is tempting to make following King Jesus sound easy. But Jesus himself never did. He did not want half-hearted half-disciples; he wanted followers who knew the cost and had decided to pay the price of living for Jesus now, knowing they would be repaid with huge interest in eternity. If we do not lay out the consequences of following Jesus clearly, then any conversions we see will be skin-deep, not heart-changing.

Q: *How would you put v 23-26 into your own words to show the consequences both of following and rejecting Jesus?*

PRAY: *Pray for honesty in evangelism; that you would explain clearly both the glory and the commitment of the Christian life.*

Day 3

JOHN 10:11-18, 24-30

Q: *Which verses describe who Jesus is?*

Q: *Which verses explain why he came?*

Q: *How do people respond rightly to him, ie: become "sheep" (v 14, 16, 27)?*

Jesus was the master of proclaiming the gospel in ways that were accessible to and evocative for his listeners. Here, he could have simply told people who he was; why he had come; and how they should respond. Instead, he painted a picture—a picture of a shepherd who loves and leads his sheep; of a shepherd who loves his sheep to the extent that he lays down his life for them so that they can live, and yet who takes up his life to shepherd them once more; of a flock who know, listen to and follow their shepherd because they trust him. In that agricultural society, every single hearer would instantly have been able to *picture* the gospel, as well as understand it.

Being utterly committed to the content of the gospel is no reason to be utterly unimaginative in how we communicate it!

Q: *Think of an unbelieving neighbor you know well. How could you use their job, or favorite hobby or pastime, as a picture of the gospel?*

PRAY: *Ask the Holy Spirit to show you how to picture the gospel in ways that will bring it alive for those you're witnessing to.*

Day 4

ACTS 2:12-41

The church is speaking in foreign tongues as a result of the Spirit's coming (v 2-6), and people are provoked to ask questions (v 12)—so Peter tells them the gospel.

Q: *How does he outline person, purpose, and consequences (v 22-38)?*

Peter does not explain the mechanics of the cross; instead, he focuses on its meaning. Jesus died "according to the definite plan and foreknowledge of God" (v 23), so that the risen Jesus can have the authority ("name") to forgive sins and give the Spirit (v 38). The cross was not an accident; rather, it was the place of Christ's great achievement.

Notice also that Peter does not mention the word "sin"; but he does describe sin in a way that cuts his hearers to the heart. Sin is attempting to stop Jesus being who he is—in their case by killing him, in ours by ignoring or redefining him. So sin is both futile and fearful: "God has made [Jesus] both Lord and Christ" (v 36), and as sinners we face him as his enemy. Only if we understand our position before Christ can we appreciate the salvation of Christ.

Q: *How would you explain what sin is to a friend, without using the word "sin"?*

PRAY: *Ask God to help you explain sin in a way that resonates in your culture and cuts people "to the heart."*

Day 5

ACTS 8:26-38

Q: *What question does Philip ask the eunuch, and what question does he receive (v 30-31)?*

Q: *Where does Philip start in witnessing to this man (v 35)?*

Q: *Read Isaiah 52:13 – 53:12. How would you use this passage as Philip did, to briefly outline the gospel (remember to include the person, purpose and consequence of Jesus)?*

Our witnessing does not happen in a vacuum, but in the context of a conversation and based on the foundation of someone's questions and frustrations. Here, Philip asks a question rather than giving a sermon (v 30); and begins where the eunuch is at (the book of Isaiah) to explain the gospel.

Philip clearly did not have a "one-size-fits-all" gospel explanation that he used in every situation and with every person. He was able to ask and respond to questions, and to point to Jesus from anywhere in Scripture. Like Philip, we need to aim to end conversations at Christ, but to learn to begin them where people are at, rather than where we wish they were at. This is not easy! Do you need to meet with other Christians to think more about this?

PRAY: *Pray for the ability to start where people are at, and lead to the gospel.*

Day 6

ACTS 16:25-34

Q: *What do Paul and Silas do, and what does God do, that leads the jailer to ask his question in verse 30?*

Q: *What is the nutshell answer that Paul and Silas give the jailer (v 31)?*

Q: *We have seen what the essential elements of the gospel are. So, how do you think the two men expanded upon their introduction in verse 31 as they "spoke the word of the Lord to him" (v 32)?*

A joyful, godly life is what leads to opportunities to share the gospel. Who else but committed, convinced Christians would spend their time in jail singing (v 25), and would give up an opportunity to escape in order to do what was best for their captor (v 27-28)? If we want people to ask us the question of verse 30, we must first be committed to living in the manner that Paul and Silas did.

The content of the gospel never changes. But the context does. We have seen the gospel being shared by various people, to very different people, in a variety of places and ways. Each person and circumstance is different; so the way the unchanging gospel is communicated will change, too.

PRAY: *Pray that you'll be able to share that gospel today, in a way that takes account of the person and their context.*

JOURNAL

What I've learned or been particularly struck by this week…

_____

_____

_____

_____

_____

_____

What I want to change in my perspectives or actions as a result of this week…

_____

_____

_____

_____

_____

_____

Things I would like to think about more or discuss with others at my church…

_____

_____

_____

_____

⊙ BIBLE STUDY

Discuss

Have you ever had a culinary disaster when making a cake or following a complicated recipe? What went wrong?

☛ READ ACTS 10:1-3; 34-44

> [1] *At Caesarea there was a man named Cornelius, a centurion of what was known as the Italian Cohort,* [2] *a devout man who feared God with all his household, gave alms generously to the people, and prayed continually to God…*

Up to this point in the book of Acts, only Jews and Samaritans have become followers of Jesus. Despite the promise of Acts 1:8 ("*you will be my witnesses in Jerusalem and in all Judea and Samaria, and to the ends of the earth…*") it was not yet clear to the apostles that the gospel was also for the Gentiles. After God gives a vision to Cornelius to send for Peter (10:1-7), Peter (verses 9-17) is told to go to preach the message to Cornelius, and his Gentile friends.

1. How is Cornelius described (verses 1-2)?

What is he missing (see also verses 43-44)?

2. What is the content of the message Peter speaks to these Gentiles? List the elements, and explain what they mean.

_____

_____

3. What might he have had to say differently if Cornelius had never heard about Jesus; or if Cornelius had been a devout worshiper of Zeus, instead of the God of the Bible?

_____

_____

_____

4. How does this observation help us in understanding our role as a messenger of the good news about Jesus? What do we constantly need to work at? What did Peter do (v 29)?

_____

_____

_____

5. Which of the elements of the gospel outlined in question 2 do you find hardest to understand and explain to others? Help each other to think about ways in which you might more easily explain this part of the gospel message to others.

_____

_____

_____

6. Cornelius may have thought he didn't "qualify" to receive the gospel. Are there people like that today?

_____

_____

7. How did Peter show Cornelius that the gospel invitation was for Gentiles such as him (v 34, 43)?

_____

_____

8. What can we learn from this for our own evangelism?

_____

_____

_____

Apply

FOR YOURSELF: What do I need to work harder at in my understanding of the gospel, and in my skills at articulating it? Are there ways in which I can be of help to, or seek help from, others in the group?

_____

_____

FOR YOUR CHURCH: How might we unconsciously give the impression in how we "do" church that some people don't "qualify" for the gospel? What steps can we take to make clear that the gospel invitation is for everyone?

_____

_____

Pray

FOR YOURSELF: Pray for an opportunity this week to talk about at least one part of the gospel with one of the people you are praying for.

FOR YOUR WHOLE CHURCH: Pray that you would grow in knowledge of the gospel, which will enable you all to speak clearly and helpfully to others.

 # SERMON NOTES

Bible passage: Date:

SESSION 8:

HOW DO WE SPEAK?

EFFECTIVE EVANGELISM IS USUALLY PART OF A
CONVERSATION, AND HAPPENS IN THE CONTEXT
OF AN EXISTING FRIENDSHIP. OUR GOSPEL
PROCLAMATION NEEDS TO MAKE SENSE TO PEOPLE,
AND TO CONNECT TO THEIR LIVES, HOPES AND FEARS.
WE MAY HAVE THE GREATEST GOSPEL EXPLANATION
MEMORIZED IN OUR HEADS, BUT IF WE NEVER WORK
OUT HOW TO INTRODUCE IT INTO OUR INTERACTIONS
AND FRIENDSHIPS, IT WILL STAY IN OUR HEADS!
SO IN THIS SESSION, WE CONSIDER HOW WE SPEAK
THE GOSPEL INTO REAL PEOPLE'S REAL LIVES.

HOW DO WE SPEAK?

Discuss

Last week we looked at the key elements of the gospel message. As you have thought about these during the week, has anything struck you?

_____

_____

_____

_____

▶ **WATCH DVD 8.1 OR LISTEN TO TALK 8.1**

_____

_____

_____

_____

_____

_____

_____

_____

_____

_____

_____

_____

_____

Discuss

Sin, Jesus Christ, faith, salvation.

Choose one of these words or names that were mentioned in the talk. Discuss how you might explain it simply to someone with very little knowledge of how it is used in the Bible. Do this without using the word itself (eg: explain what faith is without using the word "faith").

_____

_____

_____

_____

What illustration or story might you use?

_____

_____

_____

_____

What alternative words are there that helpfully explain the real meaning of these ideas?

_____

_____

_____

_____

▶ **WATCH DVD 8.2 OR LISTEN TO TALK 8.2**

_____

_____

_____

_____

_____

_____

Discuss

List three things you already do regularly that you might invite people to do with you.

1 _____

2 _____

3 _____

What gospel opportunities might there already be in these activities that you have never thought about before?

_____

_____

_____

▶ **WATCH DVD 8.3 OR LISTEN TO TALK 8.3**

_____

_____

_____

_____

_____

_____

_____

In the DVD, Erik talks about the timeline of salvation. If we listen attentively to people, we can hear them talking about these four things:

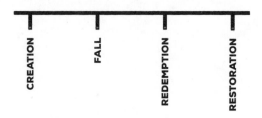

Think about the following sentences. Can you see ways in which they link with one or more elements of the timeline above? How might you move from each one to an aspect of the gospel message?

"I saw our new grandson for the first time and was amazed at how cute he is. You should see his tiny, perfect fingers and toes, and his lovely smile."

_____

_____

"When I think of young people today, I despair. They show no respect."

_____

_____

"We're saving hard for a rainy day, but you never know how the stock market will go."

_____

_____

"I'm really pleased/worried that _____ won the election. They are just what this country needs / going to ruin this country."

_____

_____

"We're looking forward to retirement next year. We have a special trip planned to celebrate."

_____

_____

"They've just made more lay-offs at work. I'm worried I might be next."

_____

_____

"Family is the most important thing, of course. That's why we're here—to bring up the next generation and see them happy and settled."

_____

_____

"We are moving next week. After a difficult few years, it will be good to have a new start."

_____

_____

"I'm spending every evening at night school. It's the only way to get ahead."

_____

_____

Pray

 **1 CORINTHIANS 3:6-7**

[6] *I [Paul] planted, Apollos watered, but God gave the growth.* [7] *So neither he who plants nor he who waters is anything, but only God who gives the growth.*

"Our responsibility as disciples of Christ is to plant and water the seeds of the gospel; it is God who causes the growth." Ask God to help you to be ready to take gospel opportunities when they arise, but also to be patient as you wait for the Holy Spirit to do his work in an unbeliever's life.

Ask God to help you explain important gospel concepts in a way that is clear, simple and easy for a non-Christian to relate to.

Pray for an opportunity to invite a neighbor or friend to join you in one of your regular activities.

DAILY BIBLE DEVOTIONALS

In these six devotionals, we'll take a close look at a "classic" evangelism text—
1 Peter 3:14-18. It's a passage in which each line has much to teach us.

Day 1

1 PETER 3:14-15

Q: *What kind of suffering does not prevent us being "blessed" (v 14)?*

Q: *Have you ever suffered for living righteously (ie: Christian-ly)? How?*

To understand any part of 1 Peter, we must appreciate the context of the whole book. It is written to Christians who are suffering because they are living as Christians—they "suffer for righteousness' sake." It is in this context that they live, work and witness.

It is natural to see suffering and blessing (enjoying a life of satisfaction and security in relationship with God) as opposites. In fact, says Peter, they can accompany one another. How can that be? Because blessing does not come from living in comfort, but in living for God. Suffering can lead to blessing; compromise never can.

Q: *Verse 15 will tell us to evangelize. Why do we need to apply verse 14 to ourselves before we'll obey verse 15?*

PRAY: *Lord, help me not to seek to avoid suffering, but rather to seek to witness faithfully, even when it is costly.*

Day 2

1 PETER 3:14B-15A

Q: *What two things must we not do (v 14)?*

Q: *What should we do instead (v 15a)?*

The NIV translates verse 15a: "In your hearts revere Christ as Lord." Every heart deeply loves, admires and worships ("reveres") something. And what we revere, we live for and are directed by. If we revere respect or comfort, we will fear losing it, and so will never be willing to risk our relationships or reputations in order to witness.

But if we revere Christ in our hearts, then we will be driven by a desire to see his name respected and his reputation promoted. Witnessing is a matter of the heart before it is a matter of the tongue. So we need to keep looking at Christ in his word, so that our hearts submit to his rule and are melted by his love.

Q: *What stops you witnessing to people? What does this suggest you are tempted to revere more than Christ?*

PRAY: *Lord, move my heart to love you more, so that your Name, and not mine, becomes what I most care about.*

Day 3

1 PETER 3:15

Q: *What are we to be prepared to do?*

Q: *What might this mean in practice?*

The word "defense" reminds us of the context Peter's readers were seeking to witness in, a context western Christians are increasingly finding themselves in—where we will more likely face aggressive accusations than open inquiries.

This verse is often used to urge us to be well versed in apologetics—able to answer common questions about and objections to Christianity that concern topics such as science, other religions, sexual ethics, etc. And this is one part of being "prepared."

But notice we're to give a reason for "the hope … in you." What is the hope that we have? It is not a concept, or an answer, but a Person. Our hope is *Jesus*. Our answers need to revolve around Jesus. And that hope is "in you." Our lives will speak of Jesus; our words may point to Jesus' work in our lives (our "testimony"). Our lives are great potential visual aids for the gospel.

Q: *Apologetic responses; sharing your testimony; explaining the gospel. Which are you strongest in, and weakest in? What will you do to further prepare yourself?*

PRAY: *Lord, show me how to become better prepared to talk about you.*

Day 4

1 PETER 3:15

Q: *What two qualities should our answers exhibit (end of v 15)?*

Q: *When we are "playing defense," why is it very easy to display neither of these two characteristics?*

Q: *What would the opposite of each of these look like? Which are you most tempted to fall into?*

Christianity is not about being quiet when we are slandered or, more seriously, our Lord is maligned. But it is not about biting back or winning arguments either. No matter how someone is treating us or how little they are reflecting it, we know that they are made in the image of God, with the dignity which that bestows and the respect that deserves. In our conduct and our tone as well as in our content, we want to show people Christ.

Some gospel opportunities will be in response to attack, some to honest seeking. In both, we must aim for the person we are speaking with to leave the conversation not only impacted by what we have shared about Jesus, but impressed by the tone and attitude with which we answered them. We want them to find themselves looking forward to speaking with us about Jesus again!

PRAY: *Lord, help me to point to you not only in what I say, but how I say it.*

Day 5

1 PETER 3:15-16

Q: *If we answer by pointing to Christ with gentleness and respect (v 15), what will we enjoy (beginning of v 16)?*

Q: *And what will we achieve in those around us (end of v 16)?*

Q: *Why might someone feeling like this for slandering a Christian make that person more open to the gospel, do you think?*

Peter is again showing us the importance of what both our lives and our lips say to those around us. In western cultures, the prevailing attitude is swinging, or has swung, from nominal, moralistic Christianity to accusatory anti-Christianity. And we should see this not as a great tragedy but as a huge great opportunity! There are more chances to show and surprise people with the gospel when those round us are antagonistic. It is far harder when people are apathetic about Jesus, or assume they already know about him. When slandered, we have the chance to point to hope and show respect. In doing so, we may make people feel ashamed of their antagonism. And as they feel ashamed of the behavior their current worldview has produced, they will likely be more willing to consider the worldview they have been deriding.

PRAY: *Lord, help me live and answer in a way that makes your detractors feel ashamed and question their assumptions.*

Day 6

1 PETER 3:17-18

Q: *What principle, which we saw back in verse 14, does Peter remind us of in verse 17?*

Q: *How is Jesus the great example of this principle (v 18)?*

Q: *What did Christ achieve through suffering for doing good (v 18)?*

Jesus is the content of our witness. He is the righteous One, who died in the place of the unrighteous, so that in his suffering he could take on and take away his people's sins forever, bringing us into relationship with God for eternity. This gospel should never cease to move and amaze us.

Yet that fact that verse 18 follows verses 16-17 emphasizes not so much that Jesus is the content of our witness, but that he is the model for it. He suffered in order to bring people to God. And we are to do the same. Christ's suffering wrote the gospel message; our suffering relays it. Jesus was prepared to die in order to save people; we must be prepared to speak in order to reach people.

Q: *How does Christ being the content of and model for your witnessing motivate you to evangelize today?*

PRAY: *Lord, thank you for the gospel. Please make me willing to suffer for it, just as you did.*

 **JOURNAL**

What I've learned or been particularly struck by this week…

What I want to change in my perspectives or actions as a result of this week…

Things I would like to think about more or discuss with others at my church…

BIBLE STUDY

Discuss

Who do you go to when you have a difficult question about something at work or in your personal life? Why do you choose them, rather than someone else?

👉 READ JOHN 4:1-30

Samaritans were considered a heretical sect by the Jews, and were therefore hated and regarded as racially impure. In Jesus' time, women were also regarded as second-class citizens.

1. What does Jesus do in this passage that makes him "approachable" and opens up the conversation with the woman?

_____

_____

_____

2. How can we be similarly approachable as people?

_____

_____

_____

How approachable are you as a church?

_____

_____

_____

_____

3. How does Jesus use statements and language to move the conversation toward discussing gospel truth (v 13-14, 16, 26)? Can you expand on this from the way in which Jesus deals with people in other incidents from the Gospels?

_____

_____

_____

_____

4. What can we learn from Jesus' example for our own evangelism?

_____

_____

_____

_____

How can we keep the way we express the gospel "fresh"?

_____

_____

_____

_____

5. What elements of the gospel message that we have seen from previous weeks does Jesus go on to explain to the woman?

_____

_____

What does he not say?

_____

_____

_____

6. How does Jesus deal with the woman raising a controversial topic, possibly to take the conversation in a different direction, in verse 20? What is the lesson for us?

7. The conversation ends abruptly when the disciples return (v 27)—and Jesus allows the woman to walk off (v 28)! How would you feel about a fruitful conversation ending like that? What happens subsequently?

8. Jesus' conversation with the woman started as she went about her normal daily routine, and as Jesus asked her for something very ordinary: a drink.
What kinds of things do people talk about in general? How might these become an opportunity for talking about God and the gospel?

Pray

FOR YOUR GROUP: Pray that you would encourage each other to be more open to outsiders. What could you do that might involve more outsiders being involved?

FOR YOUR WHOLE CHURCH: Ask God to bring seekers to you; and ask God to make you seekers of others.

SERMON NOTES

Bible passage: Date:

SESSION 9:

HOW DO WE KEEP GOING?

GOSPEL WITNESS IS A LIFELONG COMMAND TO US, AND
SO IT REQUIRES A LIFELONG COMMITMENT FROM US. ALL
TOO OFTEN, A PERSON'S OR CHURCH'S EVANGELISM RISES
WITH A TEACHING SERIES OR MISSIONAL SEASON, AND
THEN FALLS AGAIN WHEN THE FOCUS SHIFTS ELSEWHERE.
SO, AS WE COME TO THE LAST SESSION IN THIS
CURRICULUM, WE NEED TO CONSIDER HOW WE CAN HELP
OURSELVES AND ENCOURAGE EACH OTHER TO KEEP
GOING IN OUR EVANGELISM.

HOW DO WE KEEP GOING?

Discuss

Have you ever taken part in a sporting activity, big school project, weight-loss program or home-improvement project that has taken a long time? Did you ever feel you wanted to give up? How did you keep yourself going?

_____

_____

_____

_____

_____

▶ **WATCH DVD 9.1 OR LISTEN TO TALK 9.1**

_____

_____

_____

_____

_____

_____

_____

"Ministry involves different types of people with different types of gifts—all working together to advance the gospel. God gives us the privilege of serving him in this way."

How does the example of others inspire you to be more proactive in evangelism? How can you, in turn, inspire others by your example?

_____

_____

_____

How can we encourage our leaders to lead us in evangelism?

_____

_____

_____

We often think about stewardship in terms of the money and possessions we own, and the gifts and time we have been given. Think of some possessions and gifts you have. How could you use them for evangelism? How could selfishness prevent you from doing this?

_____

_____

_____

_____

We don't own the gospel: we are stewards of it. How will this impact the way we think about our evangelism as individuals and as a church?

_____

_____

_____

▶ **WATCH DVD 9.2 OR LISTEN TO TALK 9.2**

What further help do you think you need to grow in confidence and skill in sharing the gospel with others?

Over these nine sessions, how have you been excited about evangelism?

How have you been challenged?

_____
_____
_____
_____

How have you been equipped?

_____
_____
_____
_____

How have you been changed?

_____
_____
_____
_____
_____

MATTHEW 28:18-20

[18] And Jesus came and said to them, "All authority in heaven and on earth has been given to me. [19] Go therefore and make disciples of all nations, baptizing them in the name of the Father and of the Son and of the Holy Spirit, [20] teaching them to observe all that I have commanded you. And behold, I am with you always, to the end of the age."

What encouragements and/or discouragements have you had in your own outreach while doing this course?

_____

_____

_____

_____

_____

_____

Pray

"*A church that is made by the gospel must also be shaped by the gospel.*" Pray that this would be true of your church.

Tell the group the names of two people you want to share the gospel with this month. These may be the same people you have already been praying for, or this could be an opportunity to add two more. Pray for each of these people by name, that the Lord will give you opportunities to tell them the good news about Jesus.

DAILY BIBLE DEVOTIONALS

In this final series of Bible devotionals, we are going to see and hear from Jesus. We'll see his heart, hear his prayer, and listen to his call to proclaim his kingdom.

Day 1

MATTHEW 9:35-38

Q: *What word sums up the gospel (v 35)?*

Q: *How does the Lord Jesus show his authority over (a) people? (b) illness?*

Here is the King of God's kingdom showing his identity. And his teaching and healing also give a glimpse of his kingdom: a place without confusion, disease, even death.

We often saddle our leaders with crushing expectations, and then complain when they buckle under their weight. We sense we need good leadership, even as our leaders disappoint us. If only we had a ruler wise enough to know what is right, powerful enough to implement it, and unselfish enough to want to do so. The gospel is the announcement that *that* Ruler has come, and is inviting us to come under his rule. This is the "gospel of the kingdom." The reign of Jesus really is good news!

Q: *When you explain the gospel, does living with Jesus as King sound like good news rather than a drawback?*

PRAY: *Lord, thank you for your rule. Let me show and speak of its goodness.*

Day 2

MATTHEW 9:35-38

Q: *How does Jesus feel about the crowds, and why (v 36)?*

Q: *To what are the people compared (v 36)? What do you think this image is meant to communicate about them?*

The word translated "compassion" has the sense of a physical reaction—Jesus literally aches for the crowd. Why? Because he sees that they have no leader to guide and protect them. They are stressed, dissatisfied, rudderless, with no answer to the death they are wandering toward. What do they need? A ruler, a "shepherd," to guide them through life and protect them through death. They need *him*.

If we see people as Jesus did, and feel for them as he did, we will point them to him.

Q: *Is this what you see as you look at people who don't follow Christ?*

Q: *Is this how you feel? Why/why not?*

PRAY: *Lord, please cure me of any complacency or indifference, so that I see and feel for people as you did.*

Day 3

MATTHEW 9:35-38

We have seen that Jesus viewed the crowd as sheep in desperate need of a shepherd.

Q: *How else does he see them (v 37)?*

Q: *What is the problem (v 37)?*

Q: *What is the start of the solution (v 38)?*

Prayer often seems so small and inconsequential, but it changes the world and transforms eternal destinies. If we share Jesus' compassion, we will pray this prayer. And if we trust him, we will believe there really is a plentiful harvest. Jesus says there is much reaping of souls waiting to be done; who are we to think otherwise?

Whatever else our time focusing on outreach has prompted, it must surely prompt us to get on our knees more. There is great need—there are sheep without a shepherd, unprotected from death. There is great opportunity—there is a harvest waiting to be brought in, if only there are workers to do it. Let us pray…

Q: *Has your time thinking about outreach changed your prayers in any way? Do you still need to change?*

Q: *Will you commit to praying for harvest workers each day of your life?*

PRAY: *Lord, let me believe the harvest is plentiful. Prompt me to pray for workers.*

Day 4

MATTHEW 9:38 – 10:7

Q: *After calling his followers to pray, what does Jesus do with them next (10:1)?*

Q: *What similarities do you see between what Jesus did in 9:35 and what he now calls his disciples to do in 10:1, 7?*

Q: *Imagine a disciple had prayed the prayer Jesus commanded in 9:38. How is Jesus providing the answer to that prayer in 10:1?*

Praying for harvest workers is thrilling to do, for Jesus loves to include us in the answer to that prayer! We are to pray for workers, and then go out and be those workers. We must pray before we go; and then we must go and proclaim. Neither is an optional extra for a Christian. We come to Jesus by going to proclaim his kingdom.

Where is your harvest field? It is everywhere you go; every person you speak to. Who knows what harvest is ready to be gathered in? Who knows how many people have been praying for a worker to share the gospel with the people you interact with today? What a privilege to be the harvester God has placed in your particular corner of the great harvest field of his world!

Q: *Are you praying? Are you proclaiming?*

PRAY: *Lord, thank you for allowing me be part of your work. Show me where and how you wish me to harvest today.*

Day 5

MATTHEW 10:1-8

Q: *How are Matthew, Simon and Judas Iscariot described (v 3-4)?*

Q: *What kinds of followers were Peter (read Mark 14:29-31, 66-72), and James and John (read Mark 10:35-37)?*

A traitor, a freedom fighter, a betrayer, a denier and a pair of power-hungry brothers. These were the men Jesus sent to proclaim the kingdom. They had many weaknesses, but two great strengths: the power of the message, and their willingness to preach it. They did not know everything, but they knew enough. They did not need to—Christ would work through them. They only needed to be available.

The mission we are given by our Lord is not identical to the one he gave here. **Read Matthew 28:16-20.** In Matthew 10, the Twelve were given authority to provide glimpses of the kingdom—healing, raising, cleansing, casting out—we are to "make disciples of all nations." They were to go only to Israel; we have a far wider horizon.

Christ's gospel is no less true, wonderful or powerful than it was the day he called the Twelve to him and then sent them out to proclaim it. The question is…

Q: *Are you willing?*

PRAY: *Lord, make me able to say, and mean: I am willing.*

Day 6

MATTHEW 10:1-8

Q: *What had it cost the disciples to receive a place in the kingdom of Jesus (v 8)?*

Q: *How was this to affect their attitude toward their mission (v 8)?*

What is to motivate our gospel proclamation? *Grace.* The gospel tells us Jesus has done everything, and we contribute nothing, for us to live eternally under his rule, in his kingdom. We owe our lives and futures to his overwhelming kindness.

And as we have received, so we must give. Our willingness to witness should not be based on whether we think someone deserves our message, or be driven by a desire to bolster our bank balance or our reputation within our church family, or flow out of a desire to feel like a "better" Christian. Jesus is about to give his disciples further mission training (v 9-42); but verse 8b is utterly crucial. We must not evangelize for our own sake; we must "give without pay." How do we do this? By remembering as we speak of God's grace that, by that grace, we already have all that we could ever, and will ever, need.

Q: *Who can you "give" the gospel to today, seeking nothing in return?*

PRAY: *Lord, thank you for your grace. Enable me to enjoy finding all I need in you, even as I speak of you with others.*

 JOURNAL

What I've learned or been particularly struck by this week…

What I want to change in my perspectives or actions as a result of this week…

Things I would like to think about more or discuss with others at my church…

 **BIBLE STUDY**

Discuss

If you could be an ambassador of any country (except your own), in any country in the world, what would you choose and why?

👉 READ 2 CORINTHIANS 5:11-20

¹¹ Therefore, knowing the fear of the Lord, we persuade others. But what we are is known to God, and I hope it is known also to your conscience...

1. Paul has been talking about the work of bringing the gospel to the world. Look back at 4:1; 4:16; 5:6. What problem is he very aware of? How can this affect us also?

_____

_____

_____

2. What reason does Paul give in verse 11 for keeping going in outreach in? What does that mean?

_____

_____

_____

3. What reason does Paul give in verse 14 for keeping going in outreach? What effect does that have on him (see v 15-16)?

_____

_____

_____

What change does it lead to in Paul's view of other people (v 16)?

_____

_____

_____

4. What amazing privilege does Paul say we have been given (v 18)? What effect does this have on Paul?

_____

_____

_____

5. Paul calls himself an ambassador for Christ (v 20). How is this a helpful picture for us—how does it encourage and protect us?

_____

_____

_____

6. What is the result of gospel preaching (v 17, 19, 20)?
   How should this motivate us?

_____

_____

_____

7. Paul uses emotive words to describe the way he goes about sharing the good news with others: persuade (v 11); implore (v 20); appeal (6:1). How will this help us as we tell others?

_____

_____

_____

How can we sustain a passion for sharing the good news with others over time?

_____

_____

_____

_____

Apply

FOR YOURSELF: Which of the motivations Paul has talked about do I find personally most helpful as I think about being a good steward of the gospel message I have been entrusted with? In what practical ways can I live out this motivation?

_____

_____

_____

FOR YOUR CHURCH: How can we encourage the leaders of our church to keep evangelism as a central focus in their own lives, and for our church?

_____

_____

_____

Pray

FOR YOURSELF: Pray again for the two friends you have been thinking about over the course, or the two additional people you shared about for prayer in the main session.

FOR YOUR CHURCH: Now that we have reached the end of this course, pray that it would be the start of something, not the end of something.

SERMON NOTES

Bible passage: Date:

MORE RESOURCES
TO TRANSFORM YOUR
OUTREACH

UNCOVERING THE LIFE OF JESUS

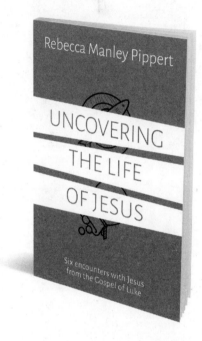

Becky Pippert's lifetime of experience in evangelism shines through on each page of these six Bible studies. They are written for a Christian to use with a group of interested non-Christians, helping them to meet the real Jesus.

This resource has been extensively used in many contexts and on every continent, and includes the Bible text. Whoever you are, it makes sharing faith with your friends simple: all you need is a cup of coffee* and a copy of *Uncovering the Life of Jesus* for each person.

*Coffee optional.

REBECCA MANLEY PIPPERT
International speaker and author of *Out of the Saltshaker*

WWW.THEGOODBOOK.COM/UL

LIVEDIFFERENT

"I HAVE COME THAT THEY MAY HAVE LIFE AND HAVE IT TO THE FULL."

— JOHN 10:10 —

Most of us find evangelism hard, but there is no greater joy than seeing people come to faith in Christ. This realistic yet hope-filled book will excite you, equip you, and challenge you to be honest and bold in your evangelism, presenting the gospel fully and properly, even when it's tough.

RICO TICE
Global evangelist and founder of
Christianity Explored Ministries

WWW.THEGOODBOOK.COM/LD

thegoodbook
COMPANY
Opening up the Bible

At The Good Book Company, we are dedicated to helping Christians and local churches grow. We believe that God's growth process always starts with hearing clearly what he has said to us through his timeless word—the Bible.

Ever since we opened our doors in 1991, we have been striving to produce resources that honor God in the way the Bible is used. We have grown to become an international provider of user-friendly resources to the Christian community, with believers of all backgrounds and denominations using our Bible studies, books, evangelistic resources, DVD-based courses and training events.

We want to equip ordinary Christians to live for Christ day by day, and churches to grow in their knowledge of God, their love for one another, and the effectiveness of their outreach.

Call us for a discussion of your needs or visit one of our local websites for more information on the resources and services we provide.

North America: www.thegoodbook.com
UK & Europe: www.thegoodbook.co.uk
Australia: www.thegoodbook.com.au
New Zealand: www.thegoodbook.co.nz

North America: 866 244 2165
UK & Europe: 0333 123 0880
Australia: (02) 9564 3555
New Zealand (+64) 3 343 1990